CHILD CARE IN RUSSIA

CHILD CARE IN RUSSIA

In Transition

Jean Ispa

BERGIN & GARVEY
Westport, Connecticut • London

Library of Congress Cataloging-in-Publication Data

Ispa, Jean.
　　　Child care in Russia : in transition / Jean Ispa.
　　　　　p.　　cm.
　　　Includes bibliographical references and index.
　　　ISBN 0–89789–390–5 (alk. paper)
　　　1. Child care—Russia (Federation)—Moscow.　2. Child care—Russia
(Federation)—Saint Petersburg.　3. Day care centers—Russia
(Federation)—Moscow.　4. Day care centers—Russia (Federation)—
Saint Petersburg.　I. Title.
HQ778.7.R92M675　1994
362.7'12'0947—dc20　　　　　94–18561

British Library Cataloguing in Publication Data is available.

Library of Congress Catalog Card Number: 94–18561
ISBN: 0–89789–390–5

First published in 1994

Bergin & Garvey, 88 Post Road West, Westport, CT 06881
An imprint of Greenwood Publishing Group, Inc.

Printed in the United States of America

The paper used in this book complies with the
Permanent Paper Standard issued by the National
Information Standards Organization (Z39.48–1984).

10 9 8 7 6 5 4 3 2 1

Contents

Contents

Acknowledgments

Sitting down to write the acknowledgment pages for this book, I feel overwhelmed. In so many ways so many people have helped me. How can I thank them all? A chronological approach will help me begin.

I will start with my family–first my grandfather, Shimon Fix, my mother, Mariam Mase, my stepfather, Sadi Mase, and my father, Joseph Ispa. Many parents tell their children that someday they will appreciate the things they made them do, and in my case they have been more than vindicated. When I was a young girl, my grandfather insisted (over my sometimes vehement protestations) that I speak only Russian with him, and that I take lessons in reading and writing Russian from him every day after school. Now I cannot thank him enough. My parents also have hugely stimulated my interest in Russian culture and provided me with every opportunity to learn as much as possible about it. Equally, if not more, importantly, they have always given their unfailing support for this and every other academic pursuit I have ever undertaken. To them my unending gratitude.

I also greatly thank my husband, Nelson, and my children, Simone, Zachary, and Alexander, for their support, interest, and insights, and for the bits of sacrifice they have endured as I have immersed myself in this project.

Early in my undergraduate career I had the good fortune to take Professor Urie Bronfenbrenner's exceptionally interesting introductory child development course, and later his social psychology course focusing on socialization issues in the Soviet Union. Later I was to become his advisee. It was he who inspired and made possible my integration of interests in Russian culture and child development. This book is testimony to the years of stimulation and wise direction I received while a student under his wing.

A tremendous "thank you" goes to the Russian and American directors and teachers whom I observed and interviewed, who distributed my questionnaires, and who became key players in the slides and photographs I used as part of my research. I thank them not only for this, but also for their enthusiasm for my work, and for their insights, which have enriched my own. The directors of the American centers were Kathy Thornburg and Beth Geyer. The directors of the Russian centers were Zinaida Stepanova, Maria Ushakova, Serafima Goldotsepova, Liudmila Kutkina, Natasha Kuznetsova, and Anastasia Trofimovna. Not only did the latter group of women warmly welcome me into their centers and try hard to answer my every question, but they also took care to feed me well. The teachers and upbringers are too numerous to list, but I hope they know how much I appreciate what they have given me. I also want to mention my gratitude for the assistance given me by Emma Piliugina, senior researcher at the Institute for Preschool Education, and to Liudmila Gavrik, inspector of child care centers for the Ministry of Transportation, for their very generous help in quickly gaining access for me to child care centers and for distributing my questionnaires to centers I did not visit. I also wish to express my gratitude to the Russian parents, some of them now friends and some of them anonymous respondents to my questionnaires, who shared with me their thoughts, hopes, and fears. Their comments have been very valuable to me.

Veronica Buyanovsky, Svetlana Mezheritsky, and Gene Barabtarlo assisted me in translating my questionnaires and the script to my slide presentation on American child care that I took with me to Moscow. Jo Ann Vogt, my daughter, Simone Ispa-Landa, and Bridget M. Austiguy and copy editors for Greenwood Publishing Group did a superb job of giving me feedback on earlier drafts. Julie Anson and Nancy Davis also gave helpful suggestions on the chapters they read. I thank them all for their patience and care.

Finally, a word of appreciation goes to the funding agencies that sponsored this research. My work in Moscow was supported in part by a grant from the International Research & Exchanges Board (IREX), with funds provided by the National Endowment for the Humanities, the United States Information Agency, and the US Department of State, which administers the Soviet and East European Training Act of 1983 (Title VIII). Additional support was provided by a grant from the Research Council of the University of Missouri-Columbia.

Chapter 1

Introduction

My interest in child-rearing in the Soviet Union was sparked in the 1960s in a child development class taught by Professor Urie Bronfenbrenner at Cornell University. He had visited Soviet children's institutions, read Soviet pedagogical and psychological literature, and talked to Soviet educators, psychologists, and parents. His descriptions of Soviet pedagogues' efforts to use group care as a vehicle for "character education" fascinated me.

As Bronfenbrenner was soon to detail in his book, *Two Worlds of Childhood: U.S. and U.S.S.R.*, the early architects of Soviet education had seen day care as a vehicle for fostering the roots of collectivism (identification with the needs of the group), patriotism, and love of work in children. Things had not worked out quite as originally envisioned, however. Educational practices originally inspired by dreams of instilling in children selflessness and concern for the common good had been reshaped in the service of conformity, unquestioning obedience, and inattention to individual differences.

During the 1973-74 academic year I was an exchange graduate student, collecting data for my dissertation on social relationships among toddlers in Soviet child care centers. During that year I had opportunities to observe informally in two child care centers in Moscow. My observations corroborated Bronfenbrenner's. In the 1970s, early childhood education in the Soviet Union mirrored the strict authoritarianism of the larger society. Lesson plans, to be followed to the letter, were sent down to preschools from central government offices. Children also were discouraged from showing original, creative thought; art projects, for example, required copying teachers' models as closely as possible.

In the spring of 1991, just months before the failed August coup by communist hard-liners, and less than a year before the demise of the Soviet Union itself, I returned to Moscow and Leningrad to learn about current early childhood education practices and to investigate parents' and early childhood teachers' child-rearing attitudes. I wanted to see what changes might have occurred since Gorbachev had introduced *perestroika* and *glasnost'*. Reflecting changing societal priorities, Soviet educators had begun calling for the development of initiative, flexibility, and independent problem-solving ability in children. I was curious to see whether and how child care staff had incorporated these newer expectations for creativity and freedom of thought and expression into their child-rearing repertoires. Were teachers and children allowed more freedom of expression, more choice of activities? How strict were teachers, and what disciplinary strategies did they use? What did they think were the most important values to instill in children?

I arrived at Sheremetevo Airport in Moscow around noon on a Monday. I had left my children and husband in Helsinki for two weeks, hoping this would be enough time just to obtain the necessary permissions for my research. I thought it would be weeks before I actually saw the inside of a child care center and was quite sure that I would be admitted only to model demonstration sites. I worried that I would not be permitted to distribute questionnaires and was wondering whether I could arrange to do that through friends. My apprehensions were founded in memories of my experiences in the 1970s, when I was allowed to observe in only two model centers, and one of them only after months of waiting.

A big surprise awaited me. I was exactly where I wanted to be—in a child care center—just three hours after my plane landed in Moscow. The researcher from the Institute of Preschool Education who met me at the airport had a taxi waiting to take me to my hotel to check in and drop off my suitcases; no sooner had we done that than we were on our way to the Institute. "It's good you didn't bring your children," she said. "It is very hard here now." She was embarrassed that she could not suggest a good place for me to eat.

Within an hour and a half of my arrival at the airport I was at the Institute, warmly greeted by people who remembered me from my 1973-74 visit. As soon as I had explained my research goals, Emma Grigorievna Piliugina, a research associate at the Institute, was on the telephone, calling a child care director, Liudmila Grigorievna Kutkina, to ask if it would be all right to bring over a visitor. Fearing that Kutkina would refuse if she knew that the visitor was American, Piliugina did not tell her anything about me until we arrived on her doorstep. "It would take too long to get you into our best child care centers," she said. "I'll take you to some average good ones."

Kutkina was shaken when we were introduced and she learned of my identity. She exclaimed that she had been hesitant to have anyone, even a Russian, much less a foreigner, visit her center; the building was undergoing a major remodeling and repair job; it was not in tip-top shape. Seeing that there was no way out, however, she led me on a tour of the center. Gradually, she relaxed. As she recovered herself, she began laughing at the situation and at her own first reaction. Before it was time to leave, she echoed the researcher who had met me at the airport, worrying about how I would find food in Moscow. When it was time to leave she handed me a bundle: some bread, some butter, and two apples to help sustain me until the next day. She asked if I would like to spend the next few days at her center observing the daily routine and talking with her and the upbringers. Of course I would.

In just a few hours I had gotten a taste of the changes I had come to study. On the one hand, people were unnerved by critical shortages of basic necessities; on the other, they were no longer barred from discussing their problems or opening doors to a foreigner. Nothing so spontaneous could have happened in the 1970s. I wondered how all of this affected child care practice.

Over the course of the next three months, I was welcomed to six child care centers. In this book I describe the daily activities of children and upbringers as I saw them in these centers. I also present the child-rearing values and goals of the staff. I have made use of both photographs and direct quotations of upbringers' comments because I think they add much to my attempts to transmit the flavor of the child care provided there. Additionally, some reactions of American teachers to Russian child care practices are presented, as are some reactions of Soviet upbringers to American child care practices.

I came by the information I report in several ways. First, I spent many days observing children and upbringers as they went about their daily activities. I took many photographs, the best of which pepper this volume, and took copious notes, writing down upbringers' comments word-for-word. Having grown up in a Russian-speaking home, I could easily understand upbringer-child interactions.

Second, I asked directors and upbringers to tell me about their goals for children, the methods they used, how things had changed in recent years, and the most rewarding and the most difficult aspects of their work. Unlike the polite but restrained demeanor of child care staff in the 1970s, this time upbringers and directors were more than willing to share with me the details of their work with children, their frustrations as well as their successes. Their openness was in itself testimony to *glasnost'*.

Third, I adapted the ethnographic film technique developed by Tobin, Wu, and Davidson (1989), taking with me two reels of slides—one depicting a typical day in an American child care center serving toddlers and the second depicting a typical day in a center serving 3- and 4-year-old children. These centers are in Columbia, Missouri; both subscribe to an open-framework approach to early childhood education and both provide high-quality care. As I showed these slides to Soviet child care staff and answered their questions, I made mental notes about what surprised them, what impressed them, and what displeased them about American child care practices. These presentations were tremendously helpful for my work. For one, it felt good to give as well as receive interesting information; my hosts were fascinated by the slides. Second, I gained invaluable insight as I listened to their reactions. I became more aware of our differences as they probed for explanations of American child care practices that I had taken for granted. Upon returning to the United States, I prepared a slide presentation depicting a day in Soviet child care. I have shown those slides to many American early childhood professionals, thus learning about American reactions to typical Russian practices.

I also asked upbringers and parents to respond to questionnaires tapping child-rearing values. I wanted to compare the child-rearing opinions of parents and upbringers and to compare them to those of their American counterparts. The questionnaires asked respondents to share some of their thoughts and feelings regarding discipline, nurturance, and the parent-teacher relationship.

Such was the feeling that one could freely speak one's mind and not worry about repercussions that not one of the people with whom I spoke asked me to keep her name or opinions in confidence. I am sure many will consider me too cautious, but I have decided not to connect individual names with specific opinions. Instead, I have preserved some anonymity by indicating, for example, only that "one director told me . . ." Optimism about the new order in Russia alternates with fear that a thousand years of dictatorship will not be done away with so irrevocably as one would hope. I would prefer not to worry that I might in any way compromise the lives of the directors, teachers, or parents who shared their stories with me.

A few words about translation are in order. In its ability to convey the speaker's affection for the listener, the Russian language is rich in a way that English is not. This is particularly true of speech to children. American research on "motherese" shows that English speakers tend to use shorter sentences, more repetition, and more lilting intonation when talking to young children (e.g., Snow & Ferguson, 1977). Russian speakers do the same, and in addition, use the diminutive form for many nouns when they speak to children. While Americans are familiar with the diminutive in regard to proper names (Billy for William, Susie for Susan, etc.), Russians can show their fondness or tender appreciation for just about anything by changing the noun ending. Thus, for example, when telling a child to wash his hands, instead of using *ruki* for hands, they might call them *ruchki*. Use of *ruchki* suggests that one looks upon those hands as cute and little, that one regards them with fondness. The tone of the command is thus significantly altered (one might say it is softened). This poses a dilemma for translation: English simply does not afford a ready way to transmit the flavor of this diminutive form. After playing with several alternatives, I have decided that writing *cute little* before nouns best conveys the tone of the diminutive. I hope that this does not make the dialogue too cumbersome for the reader.

In Russian, the word for early childhood teacher is *vospitatel'nitsa*. A close translation is "one who brings up children." The word conveys the understanding that these caregivers do more than impart knowledge; they help socialize personalities. To preserve that meaning, I have followed the lead of Bronfenbrenner and others who have translated *vospitatel'nitsa* as *upbringer*.

Finally, my English translation of the words *detskii sad*, the Russian term for child care institutions for children aged three to six, differs slightly from the usual. Others have translated *detskii sad* as *kindergarten*, and indeed the two words do literally mean *children's garden*. However, I have chosen to translate the term as *preschool* so as not to confuse the American reader, who is likely to think of kindergarten as the first year of elementary school for 5-year-olds. At the same time I have adopted *nursery*, the usual translation of *yasli*, to designate child care institutions for infants and children under the age of three.

Some acquaintance with the history of pedagogical thinking over the course of the Soviet era will help the reader appreciate current practices.   The next chapter briefly reviews the historical underpinnings of early childhood education in the Soviet Union. Chapter 3 presents some aspects of center management, including relationships with external agencies and among staff members. Chapter 4 highlights directors' and upbringers' main goals for children.   Chapter 5 explains the layout of indoor and outdoor space, and Chapter 6 outlines the daily routines in the centers in which I observed. Later chapters provide more detail about specific parts of the daily routine, upbringer-child interactions, and reactions of Russian and American early childhood professionals to one another's child-rearing techniques. The book closes with a look at what the dissolution of the USSR has meant thus far for the child care centers I visited.

Chapter 2

Some History

BEFORE THE REVOLUTION: PROBLEMS AND DREAMS

Group care for children in the Soviet Union was rooted in the dreams of social critics of the 19th and early 20th centuries. It was seen as a solution to two major problems. The first had to do with the position of women in society. The second had to do with the need to transform the psychology of the citizenry.

Despite some improvements in the social status of women in the decades preceding the 1917 Revolution, the position of women in Russia remained very difficult, especially among the peasantry and the working class. In most matters women were regarded as inferior and subject to the will of the male head of the household. In the years just prior to the Revolution, female factory workers earned less than half the wages earned by men, and they were three times as likely to be illiterate (Rosenthal, 1973). Though upper-class women enjoyed more material comforts and educational opportunities than lower-class women, their lives also were curtailed by patriarchal customs and laws. For women of both social strata, escape from a tyrannical father, husband, or father-in-law was nearly impossible.

Social reformers were much influenced by the analyses of Karl Marx and Friedrich Engels, who argued that the oppression of women was rooted in their economic inequality. They contended that women would not be valued by society or by their families until they were fully engaged in productive labor outside the home. But women were prevented from pursuing outside work by myriad household tasks, including child rearing. Accordingly, the communal rearing of children was viewed as an important part of the solution to this problem. If mothers did not need to stay home to care for dependent children, they would be free to pursue "socially productive" work outside the home. Having their own income would permit them to develop their talents and to equalize their status vis-à-vis men (Engels, 1967/1884; Marx & Engels, 1959/1848).

Social reformers were also concerned that the attitudes held by the Russian public toward work and community were inconsistent with those needed for the building of communism. In the lower classes, ignorance and passivity, and in the upper classes, selfishness, arrogance, and laziness were passed on from generation to generation. If parents were themselves brought up in this atmosphere and adopted such values, how could they be expected to teach their children something different? How could they even begin to foster cooperation, selflessness, self-discipline, initiative, optimism? Would they not continue to reproduce their own flawed attitudes and habits in their children? Moreover, there was concern about children's health. Health practices among the peasantry were primitive, and rates of illness and death were high (Ransel, 1991).

If children were away from home for all or most of the day, the ill effects of parents' influence could be minimized. Given all-day child care, children's personalities could be shaped by politically enlightened educators in the direction of the new ideals. Children's health could be safeguarded with the use of proper hygiene, nutrition, and exercise. Moreover, preschools could become centers for parent education, thus extending teachers' (and the state's) reach. The character defects of previous generations would be replaced with self-respect, self-control, initiative, love of work, and genuine concern for others. But educators would be able to succeed in this only if they had a free hand, only if children were removed from their families for much of the day.

1917 THROUGH THE 1920s: A TIME OF EXPERIMENTATION

Communal child care beginning in early childhood was thus central to socialist planners' dreams of creating a better society, and just one month after the Revolution of 1917, the People's Commissariat of Education issued a statement that preschool education is an "integral part of the entire school system." Plans envisioned widespread establishment of free government-sponsored child care (Brickman, 1972).

For the time being, however, reality dictated otherwise. The new government's limited financial resources were directed toward more urgent priorities: restructuring the economy, establishing schools for older children, and reducing illiteracy among adults. The number of preschools dropped dramatically, from 4,723 in 1920 to 1,369 in 1926 (Krasnogorskaia & Litvin, 1989b).

Commitment to early childhood education and the search for an educational ideology that would advance the new social order continued nonetheless. The postrevolutionary period from 1917 through the 1920s was a time of lively discussion and experimentation. Departments of Early Childhood Education were established at Moscow State University and in a number of institutes around the country. Ideas were shared at conferences, in seminars, and through newsletters. Experimental preschools served as research, demonstration, and teaching centers. A "museum" of preschool education was opened. It had two divisions, one focused on understanding children's physical growth and health needs, the other on children's artistic and creative development (Krasnogorskaia & Litvin, 1989a).

Initially, the search for model programs for young children led abroad. There was no desire to continue the schooling practices of the tsarist regime; those methods were condemned for having fostered social class inequalities, passivity, rote learning without real understanding, and suppression of children's personalities (Johnson, 1950). The ideas of American and Western European progressive educational theorists such as John Dewey, Friedrich Froebel, Maria Montessori, and Johann Pestalozzi seemed much more appropriate. Their views of children as inherently trustworthy and intrinsically motivated to learn were adopted.

Unfortunately, the practical implications of these notions were poorly understood and, in their enthusiasm for the new philosophy of "free upbringing," educators too often implemented extreme versions. Told to let children work as interest beckoned, to act only as "consultants," many teachers limited their input to supplying materials and arranging classrooms. Fearful of inhibiting creativity, teachers no longer planned or directed activities and took care to present no models or examples to children. Consistent daily routines were abandoned lest they interfere with children's interests of the moment. Committees of children were formed and consulted regarding policy issues (Krasnogorskaia & Litvin, 1989a).

Disillusionment with "free upbringing" came quickly. Critics accused it of producing children who lacked initiative, who were selfish and poorly disciplined, and who lacked skills for work. A report evaluating one child care center complained that

> the passive wait for interests to emerge solely from the children themselves, coupled with teachers' fears of showing any initiative, stifles children, makes them unorganized and unsure of themselves. Each child does whatever he wants, never taking the other children into consideration. (Krasnogorskaia & Litvin, 1989a, p. 261)

Along the same lines, Shatsky, a prominent educator, explained to an American visitor that

> there is nothing to me as significant or interesting as what came to us from America. But Dewey's idea of "free education" is untenable. From my experience, I know that there is no free child; there is only a child, reflecting different training influences. . . . Therefore, the behavior of the child should receive considerable social correction. It is here that we must correct the theory of Dewey. (Quoted in Woody, 1932, p. 48)

Concurrent with "free upbringing" was pedology, the young Soviet science of child psychology. Pedologists conducted investigations on biological and social influences on children's abilities and behavior. As a result of their influence, extensive testing of children, even preschoolers, was instituted. In addition to intelligence tests, borrowed largely from France, these tests included interviews with parents and grandparents about their occupational and educational backgrounds, their familiarity with various mass media productions (books, radio shows, movies, etc.), their health habits, their drinking habits, and even about such "biological" influences as the mother's age when the child was born and the time of year when the child was born. The purpose of these interviews was to provide insight into the reasons for children's performance. Unfortunately, besides being used in attempts to better understand influences on child development, these data were also used as the basis for classifying children as "normal," "mentally retarded," "socially dangerous," and so on. Placements in special groups or institutions for problem children were made on the basis of these classifications (Krasnogorskaia & Litvin, 1989b; Sorochenko, 1957).

THE LATE 1920s TO THE 1960s: DOGMA AND CONTROL

Whereas "free upbringing" and pedology did not survive the 1920s, Marx's call for "polytechnical" and "collectivistic" training was the inspiration for a set of ideas that was to color Soviet early childhood education for decades to come. Its adherents maintained that teachers, even at the preschool level, should foster concern for the group and willingness to put aside one's own favorite tasks in favor of socially useful work; it was expected that children so schooled would be prepared to contribute to society and would accord equal respect to manual and intellectual work (Muckle, 1988).

Again, however, interpretations were extreme, particularly in the late 1920s and 1930s. Even very young children were subjected to daily lectures on the virtues of communism (Sorochenko, 1957). In 1928 a debate on the value of dolls resulted in the banishment of traditional dolls in "bourgeois" dress; only dolls in workers' garb and soldiers' uniforms were permissible. Play was deemed unimportant; instead, even preschool children were given lessons in adult work skills such as carpentry, sewing, cotton picking, and sugar beet harvesting.

As part of the drive to eliminate religion, which was faulted for teaching mysticism, fatalism, and acceptance of the status quo, Christmas and Easter celebrations had been banned in 1921 (Bereday, Brickman, & Read, 1960). Now New Year celebrations and birthday parties were also abandoned because they were not useful for teaching socialism. Folk tales were no longer read because they "encourage the development of mystical religious feelings and . . . hinder orientation to one's actual surroundings." Even favorite children's stories by beloved writers such as Kornei Chukovsky were criticized for not inspiring "socialist feelings, collectivistic strivings" (Krasnogorskaia and Litvin, 1989b, p. 272).

All of this mirrored the growing authoritarianism of the larger society. In 1931 the Central Committee of the Communist Party issued a decree ordering an end to open curricula and instituting systematic, teacher-directed education. Schools were admonished to eliminate "foreign influences" and to foster obedience to authority, loyalty to the system, and acquisition of specific knowledge (Pennar, Bakalo, & Bereday, 1971). Lessons were to be presented without room for divergent thinking. Children were to copy their teacher's examples as closely as possible, coming up with the one right answer. I recall an example of this style of teaching, for it survived well into the 1970s. I had come to observe an art lesson for 5-year-olds. The teacher first drew a pine branch. The children watched, then were instructed to do the same. Children whose drawings were not close copies of the teacher's were criticized.   One had used a blue crayon to draw his pine needles. This was not permissible. Another had drawn his branch in a corner of the page rather than, as the teacher had, in the middle of the page. He too was reprimanded.

Tight control over educational institutions was to be exercised by the central government, with uniformity of goals and curricula throughout the country. Slight variations were permitted only for the sake of local color (e.g., specific dances taught children could reflect the cultural traditions of the republic in which they lived).

Attention to moral education, including the cultivation of patriotism, was to be part of the entire curriculum for all age levels; it was deemed of equal importance to the imparting of knowledge. The Russian word used to denote the process of molding the child's personality is "*vospitanie*," usually translated into English as *upbringing*.   Educators became emphatic that the *vospitanie* of children's values, motives, and behavior patterns in accord with communist ethical and aesthetic standards was one of the most important functions of children's institutions. They insisted that this socialization process should begin early. Accordingly, teachers of young children were called *vospitatel'nitsi* or upbringers, since their job entailed bringing children up in the spirit of communist morality.

Political *vospitanie* began to permeate care in the early childhood institutions that were now being built at a rapid rate. (In 1928 there were 4,300 child care centers in the country; by 1940 there were 46,031 [Krasnogorskaia & Litvin, 1989b; Shabaeva & Litvin, 1989]). Pictures of Vladimir Lenin and Joseph Stalin were hung in every room, and children were told stories designed to foster gratitude toward them and a desire do as they would have wished in every detail of life. (I recall a poster I saw in the 1970s; it reminded children that Lenin liked children to eat everything on their plates.) Children were taught to put loyalty to their country and to communism above all else, even their families. Pavlik Morozov, a boy killed by his uncle for telling his teacher that his father's loyalty to communism was questionable, was made a hero and martyr. (The boy's tattling had resulted in his father's execution.) Love of the motherland was further inculcated through songs and stories celebrating the beauty of the country, the kindness of its present and past leaders, and comparing the sad lot of children in other countries to the good fortune of Soviet children.

The development of each child's talents and intellectual and physical abilities was to occur in concert with his or her involvement in and dedication to group interests. The educator most often associated with the notion of "collectivism" is Anton Makarenko. Though developed largely in the course of his work with delinquent adolescents, Makarenko's child-rearing ideas were applied in modified form even to the care of preschool-aged children. In essence, collectivism for young children involved gradually giving up individual play in favor of group play, sharing common opinions and goals with peers, caring about the well-being of the group above that of any individual, and obedience to adults.

Most Americans, and Russians today, would be favorably inclined toward the training of selflessness, kindness, and concern for others that are integral to collectivism. The juxtaposition of individual versus collective priorities is troublesome, however. Children were to deny their own feelings when they clashed with those of the group. Whining, screaming, and other such "pointless zoological activities" were condemned for destroying group morale; children were taught to show a positive and cheerful face to the collective. They were taught to look over one another's shoulders, providing criticism and help to those who deviated. Makarenko advised teachers: "The discipline of the individual personality, and the full freedom of the individual personality, are not our music. Soviet pedagogy must have an entirely new logic: from the collective to the individual. The object of Soviet upbringing may be the whole collective only" (Quoted in Chybarov, 1966, p. 24).

Much attention was given to the development of cooperation and sharing among children. Infants shared playpens, and older children were expected to share toys readily, without complaint. Interestingly, because it was believed important for children to have joyful experiences in the company of their peers, in the late 1930s New Year and birthday celebrations were reinstituted in child care centers. These experiences were believed to develop associations between happiness and group activity (Shabaeva & Litvin, 1989).

In the second half of the 1930s, partly in response to the urging of Nadezhda Krupskaia, Lenin's widow, lessons in skills such as carpentry were abandoned in favor of more time for play. Krupskaia, who as a young woman had studied the writings of Pestalozzi and other progressive Western educators, argued that children come to understand their surroundings best through play, that play facilitates the development of organizational abilities, self-discipline, and friendship among children of different nationalities and backgrounds. Now it was acknowledged that preschoolers are too young to understand the meaning of labor lessons and political indoctrination speeches. Preschool classrooms were brightened, the decor made more cheerful. An end was put to standardized testing. The abilities of too many children had been underestimated; too many normal children had been placed in special education classes (Rotenberg, 1989; Sorochenko, 1957). The emphases on convergent thinking and obedience, however, remained.

One of the more interesting, and in some ways tragic, experiments was the establishment of *round-the-clock care* boarding schools (*internats*). These live-in institutions were originally conceived of as a way of enabling women to work outside the home and as the perfect vehicle for gaining maximum influence over children's personality development since there would be little parental interference. Research by Urie Bronfenbrenner (1970a) suggests some success in this regard. He found greater acceptance of officially approved values among boarded children than among day-school children.

The number of *internats* increased during the war years. Later, in the 1950s, Nikita Krushchev was active in promoting them as the ideal children's institution. At the early childhood level, round-the-clock (*kruglosutochnye*) groups permitted parents to leave children for the entire work week; children returned home on weekends (Wednesday nights at home were also a possibility for some). These children's classrooms, though separate from those of daytime-care-only children, were often housed in the same building. For example, a center might have three round-the-clock groups and six regular child care groups.

Children's health had been an important concern for Soviet educators from the beginning. During World War II and for the rest of the 1940s even greater emphasis was placed on health and physical strength. Heretofore there had been three 20- to 30-minute teacher-directed lessons each day. In 1949 their number was reduced to two, so that more time could be spent outside. Outdoor play was considered important because it afforded use of the large muscles and the development of resistance to the cold (Litvin, 1989a).

In 1962, the *Program for Upbringing and Teaching in the Preschool* was first published. This document assigned specific lesson plans to be followed by upbringers throughout the Union; many of these, like those acquainting children with the alphabet, were simplified versions of lessons used in the elementary schools. Later revisions of the *Program for Upbringing and Teaching in the*

Preschool reflected growing awareness that methods used with older children are often inappropriate for preschool-aged children. For example, alphabet and reading lessons were omitted from editions published after the late 1960s. At that time teachers were also instructed that teaching of concepts should occur during all parts of the daily routine, not just during the two daily 20-minute lessons (Litvin, 1989b).

THE 1970s TO THE PRESENT: DOUBTS AND REFORMS

By the 1970s an important thread of doubt had appeared in Soviet pedagogical writings. Concern was voiced that creative thinking was being discouraged by the emphasis on rote learning and unquestioning acceptance of authority. It was lamented that the graduates of Soviet schools were too passive, too rigid, and lacking real understanding of theoretical concepts (Jacoby, 1973). Since the 1980s, there has been a steady stream of writing on these issues. For example, a book published in 1990 for teacher-training purposes addresses the profound contradiction between support for individual children's talents and needs and the expectation that children put group interests first. Reflecting the dramatically different political atmosphere now infusing the society, the author contends that Makarenko was wrong to insist that the collective is more important than the individual (Nemov, 1990). Today, it is not uncommon to read that even problems in family life are attributable to the training in obedience and passivity received some twenty or thirty years ago in child care centers. In 1992, for example, a university instructor responded to an article on marital problems with a letter complaining that, "For too long we have been powerless toys in the hands of fate. From childhood, starting in child care centers and in school, we were brought up to be slaves. . . . We lost our ability to think for ourselves, to make decisions." (Avdeeva, 1992, p. 6). How ironic, the similarity between these charges and the criticisms levied against tsarist schools during the pre- and early postrevolutionary years.

Concerns such as these have been followed by curricular reform, even if slowly. In 1985 goals for children's knowledge and abilities were added to the *Program*; these goals have become more important than specific lesson plans. As long as goals are met by the end of each preschool year, teachers may meet them in a variety of ways (Litvin, 1989c). The press has carried stories on schools (including preschools) in which teachers have allowed children to ask deeper questions and to make more of their own choices (e.g., Zverev, 1990). One upbringer in a preschool I visited told me that some years ago she was severely reprimanded on the day the children were supposed to learn about fish. She had brought in guppies, not goldfish; the *Program* called for goldfish. "But," she recalls remonstrating, "they have fins, they swim, they have gills, they are fish." "It doesn't matter," was the icy reply. "You may have that kind of fish at home if you like them so much, but here you must have goldfish." Those ridiculous days, she told me with a meaningful look, are over.

The age groups served by some child care centers have also changed. Since 1986, the age of entry into elementary school has been lowered to 6. (It was age 7 before.) Many child care centers therefore serve children through age 5 only. On the other hand, classroom shortages in many elementary schools necessitate the provision of first grade experiences in child care centers in those neighborhoods.

Services for infants have been greatly curtailed. Group care for infants was rather common when I observed in Moscow in the 1970s; by 1991 it had become a rarity. Directors of *yasli*, centers originally developed to care for children from infancy to age 2 or 3, were finding so little demand for infant care that they were in the process of converting those facilities to meet the needs of older children. Why? What brought on this change?

For one thing, women's agendas have changed. Through the 1950s, many women accepted government exhortations to contribute to the building of the socialist society by working outside the home. Besides, a family could not survive on only one income. By the 1970s, however, women were according work less importance, partly as a backlash against their own mothers' experience. They remembered their mothers as tired and worn by the dual responsibilities of work and home, and they recalled themselves as children wishing for more time with them. In addition, a certain amount of political skepticism had crept in. The image of the strong woman building communism was no longer in style; a more traditionally feminine image was preferred (Ispa, 1988).

Mothers had become increasingly reluctant to leave babies in group care for other reasons also. They feared contagion among the infants and neglect by upbringers, who had to divide their attention among 15 little ones. Professional and political opinion concurred, resulting in extensions in paid maternity leave and government stipends for mothers who elected to raise their children at home for a year or more. In 1988, Mikhail Gorbachev declared that

> women are more important as producers of good *people* than as producers of fabric or whatever. I am going to propose a system of economic benefits throughout childhood for each child born so that it becomes economically possible for women to devote more of themselves to their families. The dropping birthrate and the rising divorce rate show that family life is in trouble and needs more protection. (Quoted in Press, 1989, p. 18)

At the time of my visit in 1991, mothers who stayed at home to care for children under the age of three had their jobs guaranteed and received 70 to 120 rubles per month per child (the exact figure varied, depending on the organizations for which they had worked), compared to the average Soviet salary at the time of 270 rubles ("Russia communists," 1991). As a result, the youngest child I saw in group care was 14 months old.

Use of round-the-clock, or boarding, care has also been significantly reduced. Newspaper articles questioning the wisdom of boarding care began to appear in the early 1960s. There was research evidence that a mistake had been made, that prolonged separation was not good for children or parents. Many parents were distraught by the loss of their children to these institutions, and studies showed that the children's cognitive, language, and social-emotional development was inferior compared to that of children reared at home or in a combination of home and day care (Bronfenbrenner, 1970b).

I myself remember the forlorn expressions on the faces of young boarded children watching out the window in the evening as parents of children in regular daytime care came to pick them up to go home. Yet, when at a 1974 seminar at the Institute in Preschool Education, I presented the results of my doctoral research showing heightened insecurity in boarded toddlers (Ispa, 1977), I was told by the assistant director that this simply could not be possible. Lower-ranking researchers came up to me afterward to whisper that they suspected that I was right. I had touched on an issue that was still politically sensitive.

Things change. According to Emma Piliugina of the Institute for Preschool Education, only 6% of young children nationwide were in round-the-clock care in 1991. In the child care centers in which I observed in 1991, some children did spend the night, but it tended to be on an occasional rather than on a regular basis. Directors told me that one reason is that parents are less likely to have night work now. I gathered from other comments that there is also more understanding that boarding care is not good for young children's emotional health.   There were no longer any all-*kruglosutochnie* groups; children who spent the night at the center were included in the regular groups.   *Internats* are now intended only for orphaned, abandoned, neglected, or abused children. Parents have the option of voluntarily placing their children in *internats*, but their behavior in so doing is considered frivolous and immoral (Waters, 1992). Efforts are made to find foster homes for these children, since for normal development it is considered important to grow up in a loving family (Lihanov, 1992).

The demand for daytime care for children aged 3 to 6, however, has continued. While in 1989 only about 20% of Soviet children aged 2 and under attended child care centers, about 70% of children aged 3 to 6 years of age were enrolled (Press, 1989). Figures in an article published in 1993 by researchers of the Russian Ministry of Education suggest that 86% of children ages 2 to 7 are currently enrolled in preschool or school (Tzarkova & Serbina, 1993). (The difference between these two percentages is probably largely due to the fact that the 1989 statistics pertain to the entire USSR, including the now-independent republics, whereas the 1993 statistics pertain to Russia only.) Yet the goal of making group care readily available in every neighborhood and near every factory and office building has not been reached, and many parents still complain of difficulties in reserving a spot in a good, conveniently located child care center.

This, then, is the historical backdrop for the activities and patterns of relating that I was to observe in 1991. It was an exciting time, one of transition. The old way was in question, but not all of it, and not by everyone. How did this play out in everyday practice in child care centers? How much had been discarded or modified? What was replacing it? These questions guided me as I interviewed and observed.

Chapter 3

Management and Staff

SPONSORED VERSUS NEIGHBORHOOD CENTERS

Until the last years of the Soviet system, all child care centers were state owned. Many were "neighborhood" (*raionye*) centers serving children living nearby. Others, which I will call *sponsored* (in Russian, *vedomstvenye*) centers, were established by individual organizations and manufacturing plants to serve the families in their employ. The closest analogy in the United States is a corporate child care center run by a business or government entity to serve its own workers.

In 1991 the Moscow city subway system was sponsoring 12 child care centers in Moscow, two for children under the age of 3, and 10 for children aged 3 to 6. All subway workers, be they engineers, janitors, or escalator watchpersons (employed to sit at the bottom of escalators to watch for mechanical problems or inappropriate behavior by riders) had priority in enrolling their children in these centers.

Five of the child care centers that I visited were part of this system. Surrounded by apartment buildings in fairly quiet areas of the city, each center occupies an entire building built specifically for that purpose. Two of the centers were nurseries, *yasli*, each providing care for four groups of 1- to 3-year-old children. Two others were preschools, *detskie sady*, providing care for 3- to 6-year-olds; one included four groups of children, the other six. The last was a combined *yasli-sad*, offering care for one group of 1- and 2-year-olds and three groups of 3-to 6-year-olds. Groups of 1- and

2-year-olds included up to 15 children; groups of 3- to 7-year-olds included a maximum of 20.

All but two of the centers offered round-the-clock care, in addition to daytime care, Mondays through Thursdays. This arrangement was important for subway workers who worked night or very early-morning hours.

The sixth center I visited was sponsored by a manufacturing plant, and the children of workers of that plant had priority in enrollment. It was located on the first floor of an apartment building on a busy Moscow street and housed just two groups of children; one group consisted of 20 3- and 4-year-olds, the other of 20 5- and 6-year-olds.

Why do organizations such as a city transportation system take on child care? One evening I had an opportunity to chat with Alexander Sokolov, the famous neuropsychologist. In response to my question, he referred to the need to attract and retain female workers: "If women stop working, for us it will be worse than any other type of strike."[1] Interestingly enough, however, the parents of most of the children in the centers I visited did not work for the sponsoring organizations. Most were simply from the neighborhoods surrounding the centers; parents were likely to choose a center close to home rather than a sponsored one that was inconveniently located.

Sponsored centers have more resources than neighborhood ones. In addition to the government subsidies received by neighborhood centers, sponsored centers receive support in the form of services and extra money from their sponsoring organizations. Accordingly, group size is smaller, and food and equipment are of slightly higher quality than in neighborhood centers. Directors told me that they are also able to hire better-qualified staff than the average neighborhood center director because they can offer perks in addition to the regular salary. One director explained that before, when her center was a "neighborhood" center, it was very difficult to hire good staff members. Now that her center is sponsored, she can pick and choose among applicants.

No wonder. One can readily appreciate that the perks might induce potential staff to apply, and present staff to stay. For example, upbringers working in centers sponsored by the Moscow subway system work shorter hours than upbringers in neighborhood centers (six instead of seven hours per day). In 1991, all staff members got free Moscow subway passes, free round-trip train tickets for themselves and one child once a year to any point in the

Soviet Union, free round-trip train tickets in the summer to accompany their children to a summer pioneer camp, free meals at work, occasional merit awards, and access to a bathhouse reserved for subway workers.

While conditions are better at sponsored centers than at others, directors find that it is not an altogether rosy picture. One director explained to me that the organization that sponsors her center pays for all building upkeep. A repairman is supposed to be sent over as soon as possible after she reports a problem. However, in reality it often does not work this way, and she finds herself having to use her feminine charm (flattery, some flirtatious banter on the phone, extravagant thank-you's after the work is done) to get someone to come to the center in good time. Sighing, she complained that it is very tiring to have to do this every time she needs something fixed.

Staff at the Institute of Preschool Education reinforced the perception she gave me when they assured me that, though the centers I was visiting were sponsored, they were by no means the richest or best in the country. "They are average, not at the top," they told me. Here, in this choice of centers to show me, was an example of the relaxation of the facade that Soviets had only so recently presented to the West. Centers "at the top," I heard, had swimming pools and other resources that the centers I visited lacked. The truth was that I had expected to be shown *much-better-than-average* centers and was very happy to be invited to centers in the upper-average range. One of my goals was to find out what the Soviet early childhood establishment thought was best for children. It was not my intent to investigate the range in quality among centers.

EXTERNAL REPORTING STRUCTURES

The national Ministry of Education is ultimately responsible for the curricula and health and safety standards of all centers, be they neighborhood centers or sponsored centers. Sponsored centers additionally answer to the ministries overseeing their sponsoring organizations. Thus, for example, centers sponsored by the Moscow subway system are supervised by the Division of Social Development of the Ministry of Transportation, which in turn must follow guidelines set by the Ministry of Education. When I asked a director to tell me about the administrative lines above her, she named the child care center inspector employed by the city subway system, who in turn answers to a Vice-Minister of Transportation, who answers to the Minister of Transportation.

That is not all. Child care center directors also report to Neighborhood Organs of Public Education (Raionye Organy Narodnogo Obrazovania, commonly referred to by their abbreviation, RONO). The schools and child care establishments in each neighborhood of the city are monitored by these offices, which help to coordinate a variety of inspections related to safety, health, and curriculum.

Child care directors and upbringers had few kind words for this system. In fact, it was probably the most frequent source of complaints. While one inspector was excepted by several directors as genuinely concerned and helpful, in general, directors' and upbringers' comments clearly conveyed a perception of these bureaucracies as meddling, demeaning of center staff's expertise, and wasteful of time. It was easy to see why. Regulations required that many decisions, many of them quite minor, be approved at the RONO level, necessitating that time be spent traveling to their offices for signatures.

An upbringer provided an example. One day she noticed that hula hoops were for sale in a toy store in the center of Moscow. The director of her center agreed that it would be nice to purchase some for the center. Forms were filled out. However, the director's approval was not sufficient permission. Before the upbringer could buy the hoops, she had to go to the RONO to get the forms co-signed there. Having obtained the necessary signature, she proceeded to the store to buy the hoops with her own money. Next she had to return to the RONO office to get reimbursed, then back to the child care center to deliver the hoops. Counting traveling time and time in the store, it had taken her close to half a day to complete the purchase. After listening to her story, I understood her pleasure as she watched children play with the hoops and admired her ability to see the humor in it when a little boy, accidentally stretching a hoop too far, permanently bent it out of shape.

Related complaints concerned the multiplicity of inspections to which child care centers are subject. These range from inspections of children's work to safety inspections and are regarded by center staff as bothersome and degrading. Periodic inspections of children's work require that upbringers save sculptures and drawings done by children. Parents may look at examples of their children's work but are asked not take them home because they will be needed to show the inspectors that the upbringers are indeed carrying out lesson plans and that children are indeed making progress.

Unannounced sanitary (*sanitarnye*) inspections are made once a month; these are rigorous overall cleanliness checks. They include such procedures as swabbing of children's tables for bacteria samples and inspections to make sure that children are not sleeping with their heads where their feet had been (sheets are marked "head" and "foot" to prevent this). Food inspectors occasionally arrive, also unannounced, to check on the quality and quantity of food served children. Even the garbage is inspected to make sure that, not only are children served adequate servings, but that they actually consume the allotted amount. Fire inspectors check for evacuation plans, clear hallways, kitchen safety, and so on.

Any of these inspectors may fine the centers for violations. In general, the staff of the centers I visited seemed to be doing a very good job meeting the required standards of cleanliness, health, safety, and curriculum, but the nervous laughter that accompanied comments about inspection betrayed genuine concern that a violation might be detected and a hefty penalty levied. Some of the most amusing stories I heard were about center staff's efforts to avoid being caught. Budgets were tight and directors were loathe to use their funds to pay fines. Two stories in particular come to mind.

The first involved a creative solution to the garbage inspections: children's leftovers were simply thrown away elsewhere, not in the kitchen garbage pail. The second story was about an aborted fire inspection. One director confided that one day she was caught off guard by the arrival of a fire inspector. Fearing that her center would be fined, she invited him to share a bottle of wine with her before making his rounds. Embarrassed, he said he would return to join her later, but he never did, either for the drink or the inspection. Her giggles as she recounted this victory showed how much she savored it. One imagines that she would have been equally successful at avoiding the penalty had the inspector returned to take her up on her invitation.

Fines aren't the only ways in which the external agencies exert influence on the quality of care in child care centers. The carrot is also used, in the form of prizes awarded to the best centers. The Moscow subway system, for example, runs an annual contest, judging centers according to the health of the children (determined by attendance records), food inspectors' reports, curriculum records, parent complaints, the educational level of the upbringers, the quality of in-service education provided, and outreach services.

Centers placing first and second in the contest win extra rubles that are divided up as bonus pay for staff members.

CENTER STAFF

In some ways staffing in Soviet child care centers was more generous than it typically is in American centers. Each center that I visited employed not only a director, an accountant, cooks, upbringers, and their assistants, but also a nurse, a curriculum specialist, one or two music teachers, laundresses, and night watchmen. Yet if one considers the number of adults in direct contact with children at any time, the ratio would be deemed low by American standards. For each group of 15 children under the age of 3, and for each group of 20 children aged 3 to 6, there is one upbringer, comparable to an American head teacher, and a "nanny," her assistant, whose duties are mainly custodial.

It probably should be noted that these ratios are an improvement over previous conditions in these centers and over present conditions in other centers. Two directors told me that the accepted ratios in nurseries and preschools used to be one upbringer to 20 and 25 children, respectively, and that even now, in many neighborhood centers, children aged 3 and above are cared for in groups of 25 or even 30. One director told me she was aware of centers that used to have groups of as many as 35 or 40, but she thought this no longer occurred.

As in the United States, child care staff are overwhelmingly female. The only men I saw in the centers were repairmen; the night watch staff are also men. The reason is also the same as what one would hear in the United States. Pay is low, as is prestige.[2] "Men have to support their families," was the reply to my question on this score.

Directors

The directors of all but one of the centers I visited had degrees in early childhood education, most from the Pedagogical Institute in Moscow. While one director told me that a 5-year degree from the institute was required, this information was belied by another director who had simply worked her way up through the ranks with little formal education in child development.

What were the directors' duties? In the United States, one finds many child care center directors who regularly spend part of the day in classrooms, working directly with children in a teacher capacity. This was not the case in any of the centers I visited in Moscow; the directors' positions were strictly administrative. Directors were in charge of hiring new staff, arranging staff work schedules, evaluating staff performance, organizing in-service training, ordering supplies, calling and supervising repairmen, finding substitutes when necessary, enrolling new children, overseeing the center budget, and handling parent complaints. One director told me of a new responsibility: current shortages demanded that she spend some evenings each month searching for art supplies in Moscow stores. Her devotion may have been unique; none of the other directors talked of working beyond the assigned hours.

When one thinks of Soviet organizations, one is likely to think of iron-fisted control from the top. During the pinnacle of communist control, this was indeed often the case even in child care centers. According to at least one report, typical directors were Communist Party members appointed to ensure that all staff members and all activities promoted communist teachings. Directors were very much "in charge" in their centers (Sorochenko, 1957).

This was not the picture in the child care centers I visited in 1991. First of all, I saw a picture of Lenin in only one child care room, and more than one director told me that she and her staff had stopped celebrating such holidays as the Day of the Revolution. Moreover, while the power and influence of the directors could be felt, it was clear that staff members believed that their opinions could be voiced and would be considered. Several times I heard upbringers disagree with directors over small points such as whether or not windows should be opened or left closed. While my impression was that directors' recommendations were most likely to prevail, this was not always the case and upbringers seemed to feel very comfortable expressing their thoughts. Upbringers in two centers spontaneously told me that they were happy at work because the directors treated them with respect and did not watch over their shoulders about every little thing. They described the directors as open-minded and willing to listen to dissenting opinions. As a result, staff relations were good. (At the same time, it occurred to me that these comments may have reflected comparisons with conditions in other centers; as in the case of all of my observations, I would not want to presume that they generalize to other centers.)

The youngest director I interviewed explained to me the importance of having a supportive "collective" (working group). She told me she strives for a friendly and nonauthoritarian atmosphere; she believes that this is necessary so that people will feel good coming to work and will be "calm" with each other and with the children. To keep morale up, she does little things to show respect for her staff. Occasionally, for instance, she finds reason to do their work for them. She recalled one day being told that an upbringer who is usually diligent about such matters had forgotten to disinfect the tables after snack. Rather than embarrass the upbringer with a reminder, she did it herself while the upbringer and the children were outside. Sometimes special favors are granted. These may or may not be totally legal, but they certainly work to cement loyalty. One afternoon I was chatting with a director in her office when an off-duty upbringer came in to report that she had just bought some linoleum for her apartment. Could the center repairman help her cart it home? The request was granted.

At the same time, there were indications that directors pulled considerable weight when it came to large issues such as room arrangement and permission to deviate from the established schedule. In separate conversations with me and with one another, directors called attention to differences among the centers, making it clear that they reflected differences in their personal styles and philosophies. For example, one director told me that she thinks that one of the other centers has too many toys out on the shelves, that this makes it harder for the children to concentrate. I overheard another director telling a third director that she thought one of the centers is not homey enough, that more pictures on the walls would help make the rooms more cozy.

I also listened one slushy day when upbringers asked a director if it would be all right to skip outside time so that children would not get wet. The director readily agreed with the upbringers' judgment, but it was apparent that the upbringers did not feel they could make the final decision on their own. There was also evidence of directors' clout in slight variations from center to center in the daily routine. One director prescribed a particularly elaborate daily procedure for increasing children's resistance to the cold. This procedure (described later in Chapter 11, "Meals and Naps") was followed by upbringers in all of the groups in her center. Reflecting differences in the directors' beliefs regarding the importance of building up children's resistance to the cold, other centers used comparatively abbreviated procedures.

Of course, directors' authority is tempered by, if nothing else, the numerous externally imposed rules and regulations that they must follow. Recall the inspections and red tape to which they are subject. My questions about hiring procedures brought out another area in which directors' hands are tied: the firing of staff. Realistically speaking, firing an incompetent person is impossible. Why? Because she is likely to sue, and the courts are likely to support her.

Several directors told me that they try to get around this problem by being especially cautious in hiring. All made calls to former employers and teachers of applicants to check on their records. One has a particularly creative solution: when she needs a new upbringer, she interviews twice, then tells the person who seems most promising that the job is temporary, that she only needs someone to fill in while one of her permanent upbringers is on maternity leave. Once on the job, the "substitute" is observed and, if her work is satisfactory, she is asked to stay on a permanent basis.

A third director told me that all of the upbringers now working in her center are former "nannies" (unskilled assistant teachers). Having noticed that these women seemed to have a natural gift for working with children, this director encouraged them to obtain the training that would qualify them for the position of upbringer, even offering them time off to attend classes. For example, instead of working an eight-hour day, from 7:00 to 3:00, the nanny might leave for classes three times a week at 1:30 to prepare for classes that run from 4:00 to 9:00. She would also take ten days off from work for exam weeks. This would continue for three years. Thus, little by little, this director has been able to hire a staff of upbringers in whom she has confidence and who are grateful to her for having helped them move into better jobs. Proudly, she told me that some of her upbringers have been with her at her center for 20 years.

Curriculum Specialists

Every center has a curriculum specialist (the direct translation of her title would be "senior upbringer" or "methods specialist"). Depending on the size of the center, it may be a part- or full-time position. The curriculum specialist's job entails checking over upbringers' weekly lesson plans and, when necessary, acting as a consultant to help them think up activities that fit specific goals for children's development. They are also available afterward to discuss with upbringers how the activities went and what, if anything, should be done to improve them.   Essentially, they perform in-service training.

Until very recently, the curriculum specialist was required to follow to the letter the lesson plans laid out by the Ministry of Education in the *Program for Upbringing and Teaching in the Preschool*.   Uniformity of curriculum throughout the country was ensured by the mandate that all centers in the Union use these volumes as their Bible.   Variations were permitted only for the sake of local color (e.g., the different dances that were taught depending on the cultural traditions of the particular geographic area); differences in educational philosophy or even specific lesson plans were forbidden (recall the comments about the lesson on fish in the preceding chapter). This is no longer the case.   Curriculum specialists, and consequently upbringers, now have much more room for choice as long as their lesson plans are moving children along toward developmental goals such as those laid out in the 1986 edition of *Methodological Recommendations for the "Program for Upbringing and Teaching in the Preschool"* (Russkova, 1986).

One curriculum specialist that I talked to had been an instructor in a pedagogical vocational school (explained below in the section on upbringers) before moving to Moscow and finding this position. She was happy with the change because she liked the people and was grateful that her small daughter could come to work with her (she was enrolled in the same center).   She described the work as "a big job," and indeed it was.   One thing that was making it a bigger job was that the Ministry was about to go to a new system basing upbringers' pay on their educational backgrounds and on evaluations of their on-the-job performance.   The director and the curriculum specialist were busy filling in forms on each upbringer and urging them to complete their applications.

While this curriculum specialist claimed that she liked her job, I had an opportunity to talk to a director who had once held that position and had not enjoyed it. First of all, she explained, she had not liked having no direct contact with children. But her present job also involved only limited contact with children.   Her other complaints about the job were probably more central to her dissatisfaction.   "There was a lot of paper work, too much of it," she said, "and essentially you're checking up on people. That feels terrible. People don't like you for it." I wondered if upbringers put curriculum specialists in the same category as the outside inspectors who come to scrutinize their work.

Upbringers

Responsibilities

The upbringer is the Russian counterpart of the American preschool head teacher. The two are similar in that both are responsible for taking care of children's basic needs, involving them in developmentally appropriate activities, and interacting with parents. Unfortunately, as has already been noted, another similarity is low pay and low prestige in both countries.

Of course there are differences as well. As her title suggests, the Russian upbringer is thought of as someone who raises children, who helps to mold their basic values and personal characteristics. (See Chapter 2, "Some History," for the historical background of the role.) Shaping children's personalities is less an explicit part of American early childhood teachers' goals.

Nevertheless, until very recently the upbringer had much less input than the typical American early childhood teacher in designing daily lessons for children. As noted above, lesson plans were detailed in Ministry of Education publications and filtered through curriculum specialists before being implemented by upbringers. This is changing. Upbringers now may develop original lesson plans following general guidelines concerning children's developmental needs.

Work Hours

The upbringers working for sponsored centers work six-hour shifts Monday through Friday. Typical shifts are from 7:00 a.m. to 1:00 p.m. and from 1:00 p.m. to 7:00 p.m., though some directors build in 30 to 60 minutes of overlap so that morning and afternoon shift upbringers can communicate with one another. Upbringers who work this additional half hour or hour are paid extra. Round-the-clock centers also employ upbringers for the night shift; they work from 7:00 p.m. to 7:00 a.m. Paid vacation leaves are 36 working days per year.

Continuity of care is important to directors. Often an upbringer stays with the same group of children from the time they are 3 years of age until they leave the center, at age 5 or 6. One director told me that her night upbringers always work with the same group of children and that they sometimes trade work schedules with daytime upbringers so that the children will be familiar with them. For the same reason, even though usually only two to six children per group stay around the clock, children from different groups are not combined into one larger group for the night. This is considered especially important for toddlers; children of this age are "emotionally fragile" and would be upset if they woke up in the middle of the night to see a stranger.

Unlike the situation I saw in the 1970s, even during the day boarded children are no longer segregated into their own groups; children who need regular or occasional care during week nights are scattered throughout the groups. This means that several upbringers might work the night shift in each center even though few children per group sleep over.

For the most part, daytime upbringers alternate shifts so that each one works mornings half the time and afternoons the other half. These alternating work schedules are adhered to for reasons of fairness; the afternoon shift is regarded as easier (it includes nap time) but has the disadvantage of being less convenient for women who like to be home before evening.

The exceptions are memorable. One upbringer, a woman in her early 50s, works two shifts, or 12 hours a day, every day. Why? According to the director of that center, money is not the reason, though this upbringer does get double pay for double work. The reason is that she wants the children to be only hers. She does not want them to have to adjust to two upbringers, and she worries that another upbringer might not be good enough. She doesn't want to have to "undo" another upbringer's influence.

A second upbringer, a younger woman, was also working two shifts when I observed. This time it was a temporary arrangement and not by choice. The upbringer for the other shift was ill, and the director could not find a substitute. Though tired and wanting more time at home with her own children, the healthy upbringer had to work two shifts until her partner returned to work. During this time, the ill upbringer continued to receive her salary, and the well upbringer received double her usual salary. Directors told me that this kind of thing happens fairly often because it is difficult to find substitutes. Sometimes nannies (see below) fill in as substitutes.

Pay

American teachers often ask me about upbringers' pay. As already indicated, upbringers, like American teachers, receive low wages compared to individuals in other occupations. Salaries are slightly higher for those with degrees in early childhood education. In addition, upbringers may do work that is considered "extra" to earn more; sometimes they also receive bonuses when their center scores well in a contest among centers. To illustrate, in March of 1991 one director told me that an upbringer with a degree in early childhood education might earn 150 rubles per month in regular wages, supplemented by 30 rubles for her work with parents, and another 20 rubles for her share of some prize money won by that center.

According to the directors I interviewed, upbringers used to be "from the lowest ranks," but that is changing because the job has become more attractive. There are several reasons for the increased appeal of the job. One is that more mothers are staying home to care for their young children, and the demand for child care has been reduced, resulting in more competition for positions. Secondly, in the present economy the free meals and six-hour workdays have become especially important for women who must spend hours every day in lines for food and other necessities. Also the pay has increased (even taking into account inflation) in recent years. Along these lines, employment in the sponsored centers I visited is particularly desirable because it brings with it special perks such as free subway fare, free train tickets, and so on. Finally, a sizable number of women choose to work in child care because they know that their own children are more or less guaranteed a spot in a good center if they work there; they also value the opportunity to be near their children during the workday. (Recall the comments of the curriculum specialist in the previous section.)

Personal Attributes Valued in Upbringers

I asked directors what qualities they value most in upbringers. Years ago, I probably would have heard something about their loyalty to the state and ability to transmit this to the children. What I heard now was that the foremost quality an upbringer should have is kindness. This should be above all. She should be sensitive, be in touch with each child's feelings. She should be able to communicate with children, help them feel happy, understood, and loved. She should care about their "moral education." Several upbringers told me that their role required them to be "kind, like a mother." One upbringer earnestly explained that an upbringer "must be loving, kind, understanding, self-controlled, attentive, patient; she should be like a mother. No! Even better than a mother."

"I tell my upbringers," said one director, "that if a child cries in the morning when he comes to the center, then she should think for a while, what is she doing wrong? Something must not be right in that group." Also important, continued this director, is the upbringer's ability to get along with the rest of the staff. "Having a good 'collective' is essential," she said. Of course, other qualities, such as skill in supporting children's cognitive development, are also valued. However, the more personal characteristics of sensitivity, kindness, and cooperativeness are clearly regarded as primary.

These upbringers' and directors' words are very much in keeping with the early childhood literature. For example, Komarova (1990), a professor of pedagogical sciences, maintains that the upbringer must above all have a love for children, must be patient and tactful. She must be kind and respectful of children; she must want their preschool experience to be joyful and happy. Preschool teaching, Komarova believes, is more art than science, and to be really good at it, the upbringer must herself have been well brought up.

As can only be expected in the real world, some upbringers are more indifferent and less understanding than would be desired. Parents and older children whom I met through friends (not connected with the centers I visited) told me quite a few personal experience stories suggesting neglect or active hostility on the part of upbringers. Recently, the press has blamed low pay and over-large children's groups for upbringer callousness (e.g., Petrov, 1992).

Education

There are no national certification requirements for the job of upbringer, and some have only a high school education. The directors I spoke to were proud that most of their upbringers had formal training in early childhood education. Because the centers were sponsored, and therefore especially attractive to job applicants, these directors could be more choosy than directors in neighborhood centers.

Upbringers with degrees in early childhood education received slightly higher salaries than upbringers with less schooling. Most of the upbringers in the centers I visited had followed one of several possible educational routes. Until the mid-1980s, the Soviet system permitted graduation from school after either eight or ten years. (Since 1986 children have enrolled in the first grade at age 6 rather than at age 7, adding one more year to compulsory education.) Aspiring early childhood teachers may enroll in a specialized pedagogical vocational school (*pedagogicheskoe uchilishche*, or *peduchilishche* for short). Those with eight-year diplomas take secondary-level general education classes as well as coursework preparing them for teaching. Typically, students graduate after three or four years; the amount of time needed depends on the area of specialization and whether the student is enrolled full-time. Many take night classes and correspondence classes while working during the day. Students with ten-year high school diplomas may graduate after only two years since they are not required to take general education classes at the *peduchilishche*.

While training in a *peduchilishche* is a popular route, it carries with it less prestige than graduation from a pedagogical institute. Institutes are on a par with colleges and universities in terms of level of instruction; they differ in offering courses in only one area of specialization, in this case in child development and education. More ambitious or more academically inclined persons who have finished a 10- or 11-year secondary school program are likely to prefer the more challenging coursework of these institutes. Occasionally, a person who has finished the *peduchilishche* and is working as an upbringer will enroll in night classes at a pedagogical institute. Graduation from a pedagogical institute brings with it higher pay and greater opportunities for advancement. For example, preference is given to graduates of pedagogical institutes for the position of child care center director.

Interestingly enough, directors do not necessarily prefer to hire young people who apply after having gone straight through secondary school and a *peduchilishche* or pedagogical institute. As related above ("Directors"), some would rather observe the women they have hired as nannies (unskilled teacher's assistants) and, having formed a favorable impression of them, make it possible for them to take classes to qualify for the job of upbringer. Several directors agreed that these former nannies are the best upbringers; they are more likely to be certain that they want to be in this line of work, and they are more mature than the traditional graduates of the *peduchilishche* or institute.

I found out about another route to the position of upbringer when a director told me that she thinks it makes it more interesting to have upbringers with a variety of backgrounds in her center. A year before she had taken a chance hiring a woman who had majored in art instead of early childhood education. This young woman's first job had been in graphics, but she had been unhappy in that field and decided she would rather work with young children. According to the director, she was an excellent upbringer and had added much to the center's art education programs.

After an upbringer has completed her degree requirements, she is expected to take a refresher course at an institute or *peduchilishche* every five years. The centers I visited also have bimonthly in-service education meetings (*pedsoviety*), held during nap times; nannies watch the children so that upbringers can attend. Each of these sessions is devoted to a child development or curricular issue. For example, the *pedsoviet* in one center had recently focused on ways to enhance children's sense of psychological comfort, or security. The schedule and list of topics for these meetings are decided annually, and the director and curriculum specialist prepare a reading list for upbringers. Books and articles to be read are made available in the director's office or in the staff resource room. One director told me that she prepares questions to spark discussion during the meetings; she does not lecture.

Performance Evaluations

How are upbringers evaluated? Directors and, especially, curriculum specialists are supposed to give informal feedback as needed. Formal evaluations (*attestatsia*), however, take place only once every five years. Accordingly, merit raises are awarded only that often. (Merit raises should not be confused with recent raises meant to adjust for inflation.)

For the purpose of the *attestatsia*, two committees are formed, one composed of other staff members from within the center, and one composed of inspectors and other professionals from without. The upbringer is observed and her records checked. Is she careful with the children? Do they get hurt too often? Sick too often? Does she encourage their speech development? Does she relate well to parents? Are her lesson plans carefully thought out? The committees assigns her one of three grades. Assignment of the highest grade brings a raise in pay. Assignment of the lowest grade almost never happens, since it signals that the upbringer should be fired.

One innovation regarding work evaluations was already in process in 1991. Upbringers were about to be divided into "categories." The criteria would be educational attainment and on-the-job performance. Category I upbringers, for example, would be those with higher education and superior skills. Upbringers were being urged to fill in application forms. After they had applied, upbringers would be observed by a committee. Directors and curriculum specialists would send in evaluations. Salaries would be determined accordingly.

Reactions to this plan were most interesting. Two directors told me that upbringers were not bothering to start the application process, that they claimed they had no time for it and no interest in it. The real reason, the directors confided, is that upbringers were afraid, that they felt threatened by this new system that required one to assert oneself, prove one's abilities. I was struck by the contrast between this show of passivity on the part of upbringers and their obvious interest in my comments regarding the typical American pattern of annual work evaluations and merit raises. The idea of yearly raises was appealing, of course, but having to "toot your own horn" to get them was frightening, maybe even distasteful.

Music Teachers

One of the larger centers I visited had two full-time music teachers (a more exact translation of the Russian job title would be "musical upbringers"). Music teachers in other centers work on a part-time basis. One told me that she makes ends meet by working in two different centers, since neither has a full-time position for her. Music teachers have training specific to their field; I gathered from watching them that all can play the piano and have a wide repertoire of children's songs and dances.

Nannies

Although the Russian nanny works as an assistant to the upbringer, she should not be confused with the American assistant teacher. Unlike the typical American preschool assistant teacher, the nanny does not interact with children for most of the day. Her responsibilities are largely confined to providing custodial services, some of them behind the scenes. Periodically (daily in infant rooms; weekly in rooms with older children) she washes toys in soap or soda. If the group is "quarantined" because one of the children has been ill, she washes toys in a chlorine solution and removes all of the soft toys. Before and after mealtimes she helps children wash up. She empties and cleans bathroom potties. She brings food from the kitchen and helps the upbringer serve children their portions. She washes the dishes afterward. Before and after outside times and nap times she assists children in dressing and undressing. She helps escort children to the playground for outside times and back inside afterward. She helps the upbringer tuck children in at nap time. During lessons, if the upbringer is working with a subset of the children, the nanny may watch the other children while they engage in free play. Some directors offer bonus pay to nannies who help with lessons, but such involvement seems rare. I personally saw only one nanny who actually interacted with children during a playtime.

Whereas upbringers work six hours per day, nannies work eight. A typical working day is from 8:00 a.m. to 5:00 p.m. Nannies get 24 paid vacation days per year, compared to 36 days for upbringers. Pay is low, even lower than upbringers', as is the prestige associated with the job. One director lamented that one of the hardest things about her own job is that this combination of factors makes it terribly difficult to recruit good nannies. In fact, some of her upbringers have had to work alone for long stretches of time without the help of a nanny. Upbringers in this unfortunate situation are paid their salary plus a nanny's salary, but of course it is too much work, and they become exhausted.

So who are the nannies? Typically, they are poorly educated women who think they might like to work with children. They may aspire to work their way up to the position of upbringer. Often they have small children of their own and know that if they work in a child care center, the director will probably allow them to enroll their children there. Then they can work and be near their children at the same time. (Recall that this was an attraction for curriculum specialists and upbringers also.) Some are elderly women. One nanny I met was 68 years old and worked to supplement her pension. Alternately praising the children for being so smart and scolding them for not eating enough, she seemed to enjoy her role as a grandmother figure. "Do you like our children?" she asked me.

Nurses

Concern about children's health led Soviet educators of the early postrevolutionary era to hope for a pediatrician in every child care center. In fact, many centers do have nurses. One *yasli* I visited employs two; each works a seven-hour shift. One comes in at 7:00 a.m. and leaves at 2:00 p.m. The other comes in at 12 noon and leaves at 7:00 p.m.

Nurses' duties include some one might associate with dietetics as well as more directly with nursing. They plan menus, making sure that children will get enough calories, protein, vitamins, and so on. They dispense vitamins and medications. They check playrooms and bedrooms to make sure that they are well ventilated. They give inoculations (a tremendous convenience, since parents do not need to take children to a doctor's office for this purpose). Once a year they give each child a general physical exam and a vision test, and twice each year they check each staff member's general health and test for tuberculosis. Kitchen staff are checked daily for infectious diseases. Nurses also maintain the infirmary, a small room with one or two beds where sick children wait until a parent comes to take them home.

Particularly in centers serving very young children (age 3 and younger), parents' and children's first stop each morning is the nurse's office. Here, the nurse briefly examines the child. Called the "filter," this process involves checking for fever, rashes, sore throats, and examining clothes to see that they are clean. The youngest children (under the age of three) have their temperature checked. Should the nurse detect signs of illness or poor hygiene, the parent is asked to take the child home or to a doctor. If the child seems clean and in good health, she or he may continue on to the classroom.

Accountants

Each of the child care centers I visited employs an accountant. Her responsibilities include more than bookkeeping and general management of financial records. She also orders food, supplies, and furniture when needed and arranges for the storage of these items in-house. As food and other materials are received, she helps organize them and put them away.

Laundresses

Centers also employ women who wash, iron, and repair bedding, towels, robes,[3] and anything else made of cloth that needs to be washed or mended. Centers with six groups of children typically have two laundresses. Each works an eight-hour day. In one such center, for example, one woman washes while the other irons. Laundry is washed in one machine and then must be transferred to

the other machine for rinsing and wringing. Then it is hung to dry.
Sheets, pillowcases, and blanket covers are cotton, as are the robes
that some upbringers and nannies wear over their own clothing; all
of these items are starched and ironed by hand before being put
back into use.

Cooks and Dishwashers

Up to four meals a day are served daily at child care centers:
breakfast, lunch, afternoon snack, and, in round-the-clock centers,
dinner.   Ready-to-eat foods are not used; all meals, including
breakfast and snacks, involve at least some cooking.

Centers with four or more groups of children may employ up to
three cooks.   Interestingly, in one *yasli*, after I was introduced to
two cooks, I was told that there was money to hire a third, but the
two cooks already employed asked the director if they could instead
split the salary that would have gone to the third cook. Thus, with
a little extra work, they were able to increase their earnings
substantially.   Each worked eight hours a day; one started each
morning at 7:00 o'clock; the other came in at 11:00. A dishwasher
also worked at the center. She worked five hours a day, from 8:00
a.m. to 1:00 p.m., washing the large pots and pans and other
utensils used for food preparation. (For sanitary purposes, all
kitchen workers must wear uniforms and caps; for the same reason,
the cooking and washing areas in the kitchen are separated by a
wall about three feet high.) Nannies wash the plates and tableware
used in each classroom.   This is done in the classroom; each
classroom has a sink and dish-drying rack for adult use.

Night Watchmen

I first became aware that child care center staff are concerned
about crime when, as a director escorted me around her center, I
realized that the door to each wing, and to the second floor, was
locked.   This was to prevent intruders from being able to freely
roam the center halls.   A recent article describing an assault by a
man who sneaked into a Moscow child care center supports the
importance of this practice (Stataia, 1992). I was also told that all
centers have night watchmen on nights when they are empty. For
most centers, this means every night. For round-the-clock centers,
it means Friday, Saturday, and Sunday nights.   One night

watchman told me that centers typically employ three men, two who take turns and one who supervises them.

Yardmen

Yardmen keep the center grounds clean, mow grass, clip shrubs, shovel snow off pathways, and so on. One director of a center with 60 children told me that she employs two men in this position. They work on a part-time basis.

Plumbers

Plumbers are also on the payroll. A director told me that the plumber assigned to her center stops by daily to see if there are any leaks or other problems. If a problem arises after he has left, he can be reached by telephone.

Electricians

An electrician also stops by every day to see whether his services are needed. A director told me that half of the salary earned by the electrician assigned to her center comes from her budget.

NOTES

1. By the early 1990s, almost all Soviet women outside Central Asia and the Caucuses were either students or gainfully employed; the economy clearly depended on their participation (Hansson & Liden, 1993).

2. In the United States, Hollingshead (1975), for example, placed preschool teachers in the lowest social status category. Directors and upbringers told me that the situation is much the same in Russia.

3. Cooks, dishwashers, and nurses wear white or beige robes over their clothes. When I observed in child care centers in the 1970s, upbringers and nannies also covered their clothes with robes. While robes are still required for kitchen workers and nurses, they are now optional for upbringers and nannies. Because of the kind of work they do, many of the nannies I met during this visit did elect to protect their clothing with a robe, but most of the upbringers no longer used them. Directors told me that they realize now

that some children associate the robes with medical treatment and are frightened.

Chapter 4

Top Goals

At every child care center I visited I asked the directors and upbringers to tell me about their goals for children. I posed two questions: What can society expect from a good child care center? What are the most important things you are trying to impart to children? Upbringers also completed questionnaires; the questionnaires asked them to rate the importance to them of fostering obedience to rules, inquisitiveness, and peer orientation in children.

The interview answers were highly consistent from center to center, from upbringer to upbringer. Society, and parents, should be able to expect that centers will place top priority on children's health. To that end, centers should be clean, meals should be nutritious, sick children should be isolated from the others and given adequate medical care, and plenty of outdoor exercise should be included in the daily routine. Indeed, the centers I visited gave ample evidence of attention to children's physical well-being. In the present economy, with real problems in the availability of nutritious food and medical supplies, this emphasis is well warranted.

Having mentioned the importance of children's health, upbringers and directors almost invariably turned to a discussion of "moral upbringing." Though intellectual development is by no means neglected in the early childhood curriculum (see Chapters 8 and 9, on lessons, for details), all agreed that it is of secondary importance to "moral development." Years ago, "moral upbringing" included training in patriotism, atheism, collectivism, and other state-supported personal characteristics. Now the one word invariably used to describe the goal of moral upbringing was kindness. Directors and upbringers hope children will grow up to become "good people," willing to help others. As one middle-aged upbringer put it, "Our main job is to foster kindness in children, sympathy for others, pity for their mothers." When I asked why pity for their mothers is especially important, she clarified: "Children should notice when their mothers need help. Children can help mothers carry packages home. They can put their toys away neatly so their mothers can rest a little."

Responses on the questionnaires were consistent with these comments. Upbringers rated from 1 to 10 the importance of conformity to rules (obedience, politeness), inquisitiveness (curiosity, using one's imagination, showing interest in why and how things happen), and peer orientation (showing kindness to peers and earning their acceptance). Peer orientation received significantly higher ratings than rule conformity. Inquisitiveness was rated as of intermediate importance, not significantly different from the other two (Ispa, in press).

Early childhood education manuals support these upbringers. For example, Russkova, in a 1986 supplement to the *Program for Upbringing and Teaching in the Preschool* calls attention to the fact that

> during play, during everyday activities, during work, and during lessons, situations constantly emerge that can be used to encourage children to perform good deeds and to act with kindness. Tactfully and unobtrusively, avoiding direct moralizing, the pedagogue directs the behavior of her charges, teaches them to be fair, kind, and responsive. (Russkova, 1986, pp. 4-5)

Recall that kindness and sensitivity are prized above all in upbringers as well. It is understood that children can develop these traits only if they experience them from the adults who care for them.

"What about collectivism?" I asked one day. Eighteen years earlier, on my first visit, it had been a predominant goal of Soviet early childhood education. Now an uncomfortable silence followed my question. Finally, an inspector spoke up. She had joined the little group of child care staff with whom I was chatting. "The good aspects of collectivism, those having to do with kindness and sensitivity, being a good friend—we accept that," she said. "We agree that children should learn to care about one another. But we've rejected the bad parts. Before, collectivism meant that everyone was supposed to be alike. That's not right. We must know children's individual differences and try to meet their individual needs."

Attention to children's individuality was indeed frequently mentioned in discussions about child-rearing goals and values. One director explained that "the main thing is that the staff not succumb to pressure from the past; we should respect the individual in each child. We should not try to remake him." Early childhood education books published in the late 1980s and early 1990s similarly urge upbringers to respect children's individual abilities and preferences. For example, Russkova, in her influential manual, warns that "The pedagogue should not permit suppression of the child's individual personality" (Russkova, 1986, p. 5).

A closely related theme was a new commitment to giving children permission to make some of their own decisions. Soviet educators have long touted the value of instilling independence in children, but what was meant by this in the past was not independence of thought, but rather taking care of oneself without help: being able to dress oneself, feed oneself, wash oneself, and so on. Educators now accept the idea that children should also be encouraged to think independently.

Indeed, I was to hear the words *freedom* and *liberation* used over and over again in my discussions with child care staff about goals for children. And when I read magazine and journal articles about child-rearing, I saw the same theme echoed in the popular and professional presses. The quotation below, taken from a magazine for parents, is typical of writings in this vein. The author looks wistfully at what he knows about American education and argues that children will be happier, more creative, more responsible, and even healthier if given more freedom to make their own decisions:

> What the Americans really have over us is the ability to hold steady, to be natural and at ease with themselves, to be free-thinking. The idea of democratic child-rearing finds sufficiently wide acceptance in the schools of America, so we have every reason to propose that it is these ideas, put into practice...that result in their schools, unlike ours, graduating democratically reared people. . . . Education without choice leads to the development of passivity, low initiative—our citizens of the past. . . . If we really want more creative children, we need to let them make choices more frequently. . . . The more rights children have, the more responsible they will be. . . . We should raise people who most of all value freedom and their own self-worth,

who are trained to be independent, who can control themselves, and who can, when it's necessary, relax the reins. Children then will be happier and less sickly. (Zverev, 1990, p. 5)

When I showed slides of American child care practice, upbringers commented, usually approvingly, on the freedom given American children to choose activities. I heard some murmur that their own classrooms were too regimented. Moreover, I saw changes in practice that suggested real commitment to allowing children more independence. Much to my delight, for example, I observed one young upbringer telling 5-year-old children that vases come in many shapes and colors and that they should use their imaginations in sculpting their own. I also saw several instances when children were permitted to forgo planned group activities. Usually, they watched from the sidelines, but sometimes they were permitted to choose an alternative activity. In one case, two children who were disturbing a group activity were offered (and accepted) the alternative of leaving the group and quietly playing with a construction set. The director of that center explained, "If a child shows talent for drawing, he should be allowed to draw more. If he doesn't like to draw but is good at construction, then why not let him work on construction during art time?"

Yet I also detected ambivalence. Despite their negative words about collectivism, 45% of the upbringers who responded to my questionnaire agreed with the statement, "I want the children in my group to put the group's interests above their own." (In comparison, only 11% of American early childhood teachers agreed with this statement.) It was also very interesting to see subtle discrepancies between these professionals' interpretation of "freedom of choice" and those of Americans. For example, one upbringer of 5- and 6-year-olds, when telling me that she thinks children should be given more freedom, commented that "children should be allowed to not want to do something today; maybe they'll want to do it tomorrow." I wondered if, in her mind, freedom was limited to deciding *when* to participate in an activity. How would she feel if a child *never* agreed to involve himself in a particular project?

Another upbringer indicated mixed feelings about the art activities depicted in my American slides. (The slides show some typical American preschool scenes of "messy" art activities, with children having complete freedom to decide what to paint and how to go about it.) She commented that children need first to be taught how to represent their world. Later, after they have learned enough to incorporate these lessons into their "free" work, they can be allowed to draw as they wish. Most art activities that I observed were in fact planned in accord with this belief; children were to try to copy upbringers' examples.

Furthermore, during meals, children were served their portions rather than serving themselves. When I mentioned that American children usually serve themselves, upbringers expressed some distrust in children's natural inclinations. They were concerned that one child might take too much, leaving too little for the others. Or children might take only one food, not giving themselves a balanced meal.

During free playtimes, children did indeed choose materials, but upbringers tended to direct dramatic play, telling children exactly what they should do next. I took notes during two illustrative doctor play episodes. The episodes took place in two different centers, with two different upbringers. In the first instance, an upbringer noticed that some children were bent over a doll, pretending that she was sick. The upbringer first looked for a uniform for the "doctor." The barber's apron that the child was wearing would not do. Having found the appropriate attire for her, the upbringer proceeded to tell her exactly what to say and what to do. "Turn her [the doll] around. Listen to how she's breathing. Take her temperature. This is medicine you must give. Give the doll a tablet so she'll feel better. Good girl." In another center, a child wanted to be a mother tending to her sick child. This upbringer was equally active. "Now open your equipment case. Good. Listen to her [the doll's] little chest. Put cups on her [a reference to a traditional Russian practice of putting small warm bottles on the chest of persons with respiratory illnesses]. You're the mother. Nowadays mothers have to be able to do everything" [alluding to the recent national decline in the availability of professional medical care]. The upbringer, not the child, was doing the thinking.

The ways in which upbringers handled children's quarrels were also very interesting in this regard. The "problem-solving" or "social skills training" approach is popular in the United States. Adherents try to help children generate and evaluate a variety of solutions to their interpersonal conflicts. For example, quarreling children might be asked to think about their two differing perspectives on the cause of the conflict, to propose some solutions, to choose one that might work, to try it, and then to think about whether it was a good solution. The goal is to teach children how to handle conflicts fairly and *on their own* (Urbain & Kendall, 1980).

In Moscow, I was at first surprised to see that many squabbles were simply ignored. Probably I should not have been, given the upbringer to child ratio of 1:20. In a way, one might see some fostering of independence here, since many times the children did settle their problems amicably without adult intervention. However, I am convinced that this was not a deliberate strategy, since one of upbringers' biggest complaints about their working conditions was that the adult to child ratio makes it impossible to properly attend to children.

Adults do intervene when a conflict appears to be getting out of hand. The typical pattern seemed to be for the upbringer to offer a solution and for the children to accept her idea. Arguments were thus settled quickly. For example, when children squabbled over toys, upbringers usually pointed out to them that they need not fight, since there were more of the same type of toy in the room. I was taking notes when two boys started quarreling over a riding toy; one boy hit the other on the head. "Misha and Andriusha, why are you fighting?" questioned the upbringer. Not waiting for an answer, she offered a way out of the predicament: "We have other cars. Go get another one."

When children complained of being hurt by another child, the upbringer would often ask the other child, "Was it an accident?" Of course the answer was more often than not in the affirmative, allowing the upbringer to let the matter drop with a brief admonition to be more careful.

Many more examples of upbringers' strategies for handling disagreements are offered in Chapter 12 ("Discipline"). For now, the important point is that children are not taught how to think about their problems so that they might learn to resolve differences on their own. Children might learn how to settle their differences by trial and error, or by attending to the examples offered by upbringers, but there is no systematic effort to train them to do so. Upbringers have the solutions. Children accept them.

This brings up a related point. None of the directors or upbringers explicitly mentioned the teaching of obedience as one of their goals. In fact, one might think that the new emphases on freedom and individual development might run counter to a desire to foster obedience in children. Yet children were clearly given messages indicating its importance. Note the following episode as one example.

It was 4:15 in the afternoon and the children were told to gather around the upbringer for a surprise. It was Dima's fifth birthday, and the upbringer wanted to congratulate him and wish him well. Very warmly, she exclaimed, "Look at how handsome our cute little Dima looks! Look how well-dressed he is today. Let's give him this book as a present. Let's congratulate him. Let's wish him to grow up to be big and *obedient* [emphasis mine] and a good student." Next Dima made the rounds, giving each child and adult in the room a jelly-filled pastry. Though Dima seemed surefooted enough to me, the upbringer hovered over him, afraid he might drop the plate and break it. As an outsider looking in, I was struck by the warmth of the interaction, but also by the combination of the wish for "obedience" and the lack of faith in Dima's capability to safely deliver his treats by himself.

Politeness also was never explicitly mentioned as a goal for child rearing, but time and again I saw that it was in fact valued very much. Whenever I entered a classroom, children were asked to stop what they were doing to greet me. Their friendly smiles as they did so were charming indeed, and very welcoming. They were reminded to say please when asking me to join them, and to use the polite form of "you."[1] The teaching of manners was especially in evidence during mealtimes. Upbringers and others who happened to enter the room wished children "pleasant appetites" at the beginning of meals, and the children were expected to respond with "thank you." While eating, children are reminded over and over to eat neatly and politely (hold your spoon in one hand, your bread in the other; bow your head over your bowl; do not slurp; stay seated until you have finished chewing). After finishing meals, children were to wipe their mouths, make eye contact with the upbringer or nanny while thanking her for the food, and take their dirty dishes to a designated spot near the adult sink (where they would be washed by the nanny). Children who forgot to say thank you were asked to return to the table to do so.

Neatness is also highly valued, and often mentioned in conjunction with politeness and "aesthetic education," or the fostering of good taste and appreciation for beauty (e.g., Zvorigina, 1988). Children are trained early to be tidy, to care about their own appearance and that of their surroundings. This was clearly demonstrated one day as an upbringer prepared to escort children to the music room. First she checked her classroom to make sure it was tidy; having satisfied herself that it was, she proceeded to concern herself with the children's appearance. Reminding them to tuck in their shirts and blouses, she exclaimed, "We can't go in the corridor looking sloppy! We must always be neat and polite." As upbringers prepare to begin a lesson, they often alert the children that they should "sit straight and pretty and listen carefully." The mealtime admonitions described above, the time spent straightening children's clothes and combing girls' hair after nap time, and the neatness and attractiveness of almost every room I visited also reflect these concerns.

In sum, interesting tensions exist in these centers between the old and the emerging philosophies of child-rearing. These are, of course, the same tensions that today permeate the entire society, leaving people confused about the meaning, and even the value, of freedom and respect for individual differences. As Sergei Parsadanian wrote in his article for parents, the issue is particularly acute for children and the elderly:

> The ideological values we lived by for the past 70 years are being revised and reevaluated. Time will tell which ones will prove to be lasting in the conditions of freedom of speech and liberation of the spirit. But the process is very difficult for everyone, especially for the children and for the elderly. One (the child) enters life with great gaps in morality and ideology. These gaps, with incredible ease, may become filled with God knows what. The others (the elderly) may leave life with the painful feeling that the house they were building for decades is on fire and it is not only not being saved, but that all the time more dry twigs are being thrown on it. In fact they are right. (1990, p. 3)

The centers in which I observed seem to be charting a conservative course, gradually allowing children and upbringers a little more freedom while still maintaining a good deal of structure. Their careful approach is probably wise. I am reminded of a 1990 article in which some teachers are criticized for implementing a "false democracy." One example involved asking children to vote on whether or not $3 + 2 = 4$ (Zverev, 1990). Until appropriate limits of freedom are better understood, and workable strategies for implementation are tested, children are likely to be better off in a slowly evolving system than in one that makes swift, radical changes.

NOTE

1. Russian, like many other languages, has a familiar and a polite form of the word *you*.

Chapter 5

Space and Equipment

One- and two-story freestanding buildings house centers in which care is provided for four to six groups of children. The smaller center I visited, in which care is provided for only two groups of children, is located on the first floor of an apartment building. The descriptions in this chapter are based primarily on the indoor and outdoor spaces of the larger centers. Directors' comments and my reading of the Soviet early childhood literature lead me to believe that the physical arrangements I saw in these centers were quite typical. Yet it is important to note that, although there are many similarities across centers, indoor and outdoor spaces are not identical across or even within centers. As will become evident below, within certain guidelines, directors and upbringers may express personal tastes and values in room decor and selection and arrangement of equipment.

OUTDOOR PLAY AREAS

Each center has a fenced-in outdoor play area. These are likely to be similar to American early childhood playgrounds in their climbing equipment, sandboxes, and trails for tricycle riding. They are very different from American outdoor play areas, however, in two regards.

First, each group has its own play area separate from those of the other groups. The different groups of children do not mix. Second, each of these separate play areas has a small wooden shelter in it. As can be seen from Photograph 1, these shelters typically include three walls and a roof; one side is open.

Photograph 1. Each group has its own outdoor play space and shelter.

Why is the play area divided? It is a preventative measure, designed to safeguard children from the germs of children in the other groups. It is believed that keeping the groups as separate as possible minimizes the spread of communicable diseases. Indeed, one director showed me that each group in her center has a separate door and hallway into the building. In addition, there is a separate exit/entrance reserved for sick children only. Directors of centers with fewer entrances envied this arrangement.

The shelters are also important. Breathing fresh air and acclimating to the cold are considered vital to good health. Unless temperatures are really frigid (-15° Centigrade for 2-year-olds, -18° Centigrade for 3- and 4-year-olds, and -20° Centigrade for 5- and 6-year-olds),[1] children are outside every day for an hour and a half to two hours in the morning and again for the same amount of time in the late afternoon. The shelters are also useful for briefly escaping snow in the winter and the hot sun in the summer. In warm weather, a heavy rain might send groups indoors, but drizzles are waited out in the shelters. When it is drizzling or snowing hard, or when the ground is slushy, games such as "catch the rabbit" are played in the shelters. (See Chapter 10, "Outside Time" for detailed descriptions of outdoor activities.)

INDOOR SPACES

By American standards, the centers I visited were spacious. Whereas each American group of children is likely to have a classroom and a bathroom at its disposal, each Russian group occupies a complex of four rooms: a playroom, a dressing room, a bedroom, and a bathroom. In addition, there are usually one or two large rooms used by all of the groups in the center for music activities and physical education. Each center also includes offices for the director, the nurse, and the accountant, a kitchen, a laundry room, and a staff room that is used for meetings and storage of toys and pedagogical books. The descriptions in this chapter will focus on those rooms actually used by children: the playrooms, dressing rooms, bedrooms, bathrooms, and music and gym rooms.

The Dressing Room

Each day, the first and last room the child sees in the center is the dressing room. To get to the playroom, one must go through this room. Dressing rooms are lined with 20 child-sized wooden closets, one for each child. These closets are about one foot wide and four feet tall, similar to the cubbies typically found in American preschool classrooms except that each has a door. Inside the closets are children's outdoor and extra clothing. The doors ensure that the dressing room will look neat even when the closets are full. So that children can easily identify their own closets, each door is decorated with a different picture or letter.

Long benches run down the center of the dressing rooms. Children and upbringers sit on these while putting on and taking off jackets, leggings, boots, and so on. No outerwear, including boots or shoes worn outdoors, is permitted in the playroom. So that floors will stay clean, children change into light shoes worn only indoors before entering the playroom.

In most centers children's sculptures, drawings, and paintings are displayed either directly on top of the closets, on the wall above, or on a separate shelf hung on the wall above the closets. Handwritten signs explain the purpose of the lessons that led to these works. The displays are for parents, who may view them in the morning when they bring their children to the center, and in the evening when they pick them up. Children's art does not go home. Upbringers must save it as evidence for the inspectors to show that they have been developing and following appropriate lesson plans. In answer to my question, "What do you do if parents really want to have one of their children's drawings or sculptures?" one director shrugged her shoulders and replied, "Well, if they want it badly, we'll let them have it." I inferred that this just didn't happen; parents knew the expectations well, and it did not occur to them to ask.

Parenting books and signs for parents also occupy the space above the closets. Parents may borrow the books. The signs are hand-lettered by center staff. Some advise parents about the daily routine at the center and ask them to maintain it on weekends. Some warn about common household dangers or give ideas about exercises and other activities to share with children.

The dressing room thus has two functions; it is a place where children dress into and out of outdoor clothing, and it is a place for communications to parents. Indeed, it is the only room of the class-

Photograph 2. A father helps his son change from winter outerwear to indoor play clothing. They will say their good-byes here, in the dressing room.

room complex that parents are permitted to enter on a regular basis. They are not permitted into the playroom for fear that their street shoes will dirty the floor. In the morning it is in the dressing room that parents bid their children good-bye for the day. If children are not outside when parents come to pick them up, then it is from the dressing room that parents lean (but do not step) into the playroom to let their children know that it is time to go home.

Photograph 2 shows a father and his son in a dressing room. The father is helping his son put on his indoor shoes. Note in the background the closets marked with individual letters. Information for parents is on top of and above the closets.

The Playroom

The playroom is typically a large rectangular room, about 2,000 square feet in area. Walls are painted off-white, light blue-gray, or light yellow. Windows are large; Russians believe that natural sunlight is very important for health. "Daylight, which includes in its spectrum ultraviolet rays, promotes the preservation of vision, creates the prerequisite conditions for industriousness and positive emotions in children, and also improves the quality of the surrounding air" (Bogina & Terekhova, 1987, p. 81). In our conversations, directors expressed the same sentiments.

"Aesthetic education," fostering good taste and teaching children to enjoy beauty in their surroundings as well as in the arts, requires that playrooms and equipment be attractive and neatly arranged. A variety of details provide evidence of upbringers' efforts in this regard. For example, windows are covered with curtains, often pretty, lacy ones sewn by staff members. Potted plants sit on windowsills. Although practical considerations dictate the use of linoleum for floors, housekeeping areas boast area rugs with Oriental designs. Professionally produced pictures of animals or Russian folk scenes decorate the walls in some rooms. (I did not see art produced by children on the walls in any of the playrooms I visited.) Toys are neatly arranged and organized by type (e.g., pencils and paper together, small manipulatives together, and so on). Dolls are prettily dressed and neatly groomed.

Most of the playroom space is devoted to five interest areas: housekeeping, block, small manipulative, drawing, and reading. These areas are readily identifiable by the items on the shelves and by other equipment in the vicinity. Each playroom also has an adult-sized desk for upbringers' use and a nearby storage closet for items off-limits to children. Most playrooms also include a small area from which meals are served and in which dishes are washed and drained; an adult-sized sink, a dish drainer, and one or two serving tables suffice. (In one center the sink and drainer were in a small adjacent room).

The block area is usually carpeted, so that children will feel comfortable sitting on the floor to build. Blocks are wooden and painted in bright colors. By American standards they are small; the longest are about a foot long. They come in a variety of shapes: squares, rectangles, cylinders, triangles, and arches. Small toy cars and animals are available for use with blocks. In many playrooms pull toys (such as chickens that peck as they roll) and riding toys are also stored in this area.

In keeping with the great importance accorded role play (Zvorigina, 1988), the housekeeping area is particularly prominent and elaborately equipped. Shelves contain empty food containers and toy pots, pans, dishes, and telephones. Toy furniture includes at minimum a doll-sized bed, a child-sized stove, and a child-sized table and chairs for four. Doll beds are usually covered with frilly pink or white bedspreads. The table and matching chairs are often lacquered, decorated in Russian folk motif. Some have tablecloths. In almost every room, a toy samovar and/or a tea set grace the tables. Pretty plastic dolls sit on the chairs. Oriental-style rugs enhance the eye appeal of these areas. Photograph 3 shows some of these details.

Other housekeeping props differ from room to room. For example, the housekeeping area in one room contained a large bathtub for dolls (a small child could have fit in it), a mechanical swing for dolls, and a child-sized refrigerator. The upbringers in another playroom had set up a small salon for hairdressing. A child-sized ironing board with iron stood near the toy stove. Note, in Photograph 3, the "television" painted on a cardboard box, the pretend piano, and the vanity table with mirror and empty cosmetic containers. Children in this room also had access to miniature doll house-size furniture.

The area where small manipulatives are kept is often in a corner of the playroom. It is marked by one or two small tables (each with seating for two or four children) and shelves with a variety of items. Some examples of manipulatives include pegs with pegboards, nesting cups, graduated rings to fit on poles, Lego-like construction sets, lacing boards, and matching games. I was surprised to see no puzzles; upbringers told me that the one I brought with me was the

Photograph 3. A boy plays with a doll in the housekeeping area. Note the Oriental-style rug; the table with tablecloth, tea set, and toy telephone; the frilly bedspread on the doll bed; and the stiff but well-groomed, well-dressed dolls.

first one they had ever seen. Many of the manipulatives are handmade by center staff and parents. Most are fashioned from thin plywood and colorfully painted. The directors who showed me the handmade toys in their centers were justly proud of their collections.

A modest art area is likely to be next to the area with small manipulatives. In the centers I visited, this area consisted of one small table with colored pencils, paper, and sometimes crayons and plasticine (a clay-like non-hardening modeling material). Paints are used only during upbringer-led lessons; they are not left out for independent free time use.

The reading area is usually defined by a shelf holding several (usually no more than five) children's books. Children stand at the shelf or sit nearby while they leaf through them.

In many American classrooms, shelves extend at right angles from the walls; they are used as dividers to separate the various areas from one another. This was not the case in any of the Moscow centers when I visited. With only one upbringer for 15 to 20 children, greater visibility across the playroom is needed. All shelving is on the perimeter of the playroom. Most toys are within children's reach, but some items are too high and must be brought down by an upbringer. One director mentioned that she had heard that in America it is thought that all toys within sight of children should also be within their reach. I told her that she was correct and explained the rationale for the "American position"; having toys within children's reach is believed to promote independence and to reduce frustration. She disagreed with this concept. One manual for upbringers explains why: "It is best if [complicated didactic toys] are on shelves taller than the children so that an adult is in a position not only to help reach these toys, but also to supervise children's play with them" (Zvorigina, 1988, p. 93).

In addition to the areas described above, all playrooms have tables for use during lessons and meals. (In one center, these tables were in small rooms adjacent to the playrooms, but this was unusual.) This furniture is in addition to the small tables in the housekeeping and manipulatives areas. According to one early childhood education manual, tables for 2- to 4-year-olds should seat four children; tables for 5- and 6-year- olds should seat two (Bogina & Terekhova, 1987). In most of the playrooms for 2- to 4-year-olds that I visited, there were indeed five square tables, each with seating for four children. Photograph 4, taken during an art lesson, shows this preferred arrangement. Though this may be the ideal,

Photograph 4. Tables that seat four are preferred for children under the age of five. This photograph was taken during an art lesson.

there were also some playrooms in which tables were larger, with room for six to eight. Most tables are plain but serviceable. One director, however, was very proud that she had managed to order the ones for her center from what were then the Baltic republics. They were painted orange. In another center, similar ones were painted green.

I did not observe in many playrooms for 5- and 6-year-olds. Those few that I did visit conformed to the preferred school-like pattern of having tables for two arranged in three rows. Children sit next to each other, rather than across from each other, so that they can see the upbringer during lessons.

Figures 5.1 and 5.2 show the layout in two of the playrooms in which I observed. Both are for 3- and 4-year-olds. Neither are drawn to scale, but they will give the reader an idea of the types of items present in playrooms and their arrangement.

The Bathroom

Each group has its own bathroom. These differ from typical American early childhood center bathrooms in four respects. First, while all bathrooms are equipped with child-sized toilets and sinks, those for children aged 3 and under also have shelves with potties, one for each child. Potties resemble large metal cups with handles (see Photograph 5). Each potty has a number painted on it and its own separate cubicle on the shelves. This is to prevent the spread of disease. It is the nanny's job to clean the potties after each use.

Toilet training begins at eight months, as soon as infants can sit independently. The upbringer or nanny seats each infant or toddler on the potty at regular intervals. Children wear diapers until they are eighteen months old and are expected to start asking for the potty when they are two years old. (One director told me that children will develop nephritis, a kidney inflammation, if they wear diapers any longer.) Until children are about three years of age, they use the potties. Three-year-olds have a choice between using a potty or the toilet; 4-year-olds use toilets only.

The second way in which these bathrooms differ from what one typically sees in the United States is in the arrangement for towels. Disposable paper towels are rare. Instead, each child has his or her own cloth towel. These are hung on pegs in small individual cubicles. Each child knows which cubicle is his or hers. As can be seen in Photograph 6, despite the attempt to construct the cubicles in such as way as to separate each child's towel from other

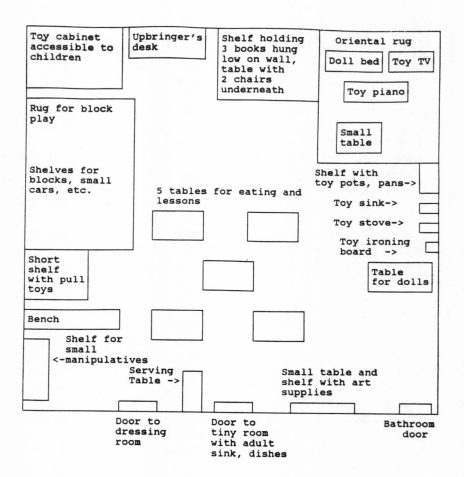

Figure 5.1. The layout of one playroom for 3- and 4-year-olds.

62

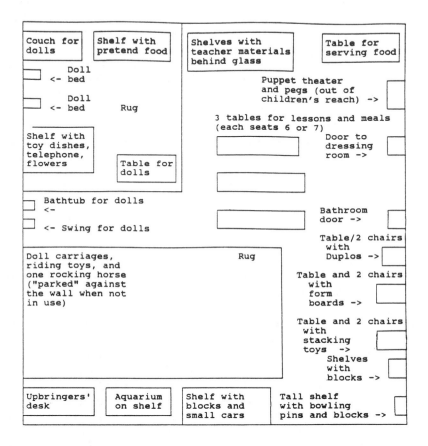

Figure 5.2. The layout in another playroom for 3- and 4-year-olds.

children's, towels in adjacent cubicles do inevitably come into contact with one another. Individual cups with toothbrushes may rest on top of the towel cubicles. (In some centers, toothbrushes hang on hooks on the wall.)

Third, some bathrooms have a row of combs hung on pegs in a line on the wall. In other centers combs are kept on the top of the towel cubicles. Each child has a comb supplied by parents. Given the emphasis put on neatness, it may not be surprising that children's (especially girls') hair is combed after nap time.

And finally, the fourth item of note in bathrooms is a fixture that looks like a small bathtub or shower stall. It is equipped with running water and is used especially in the summer after outside time. In the summer, after children play outside, their feet and legs are washed here, so that they will be clean for meal- and nap times.

The Bedroom

Though not all centers in Russia have separate rooms where children sleep, a great many do. These rooms adjoin the playroom. Upbringers and directors were shocked to learn that in the Child Development Laboratory of the University of Missouri, which has been rated by *Child* magazine one of the best in the United States (Black, 1992), children nap on cots scattered around the classroom. "They can't possibly get adequate sleep this way!" exclaimed more than one upbringer. Cozy beds are considered essential to the deep sleep children need in the middle of the day.

And cozy their beds are. Each child has an assigned child-sized wooden bed with a headboard and a footboard, starched cotton sheets, big pillows covered with starched cotton pillow cases, and woolen blankets protected by starched cotton blanket covers. The cotton bedding is laundered each week, or more frequently if necessary. For sanitary reasons, sheets are marked "head" and "foot" so that children will not put their heads where their were feet before. (Inspectors will fine the center if they find a child sleeping with his or her head at the "foot end" of the bed.) In all but one of the centers I visited, the direction of the bedding on neighboring beds is alternated so that children will not bother one another during nap time. This head-foot arrangement is shown in Photograph 7. One director had managed to buy ultraviolet lights for the bedrooms in her center. She explained that these were used as disinfectants. They were turned on for a few minutes before children came in. Another director, envious of this purchase,

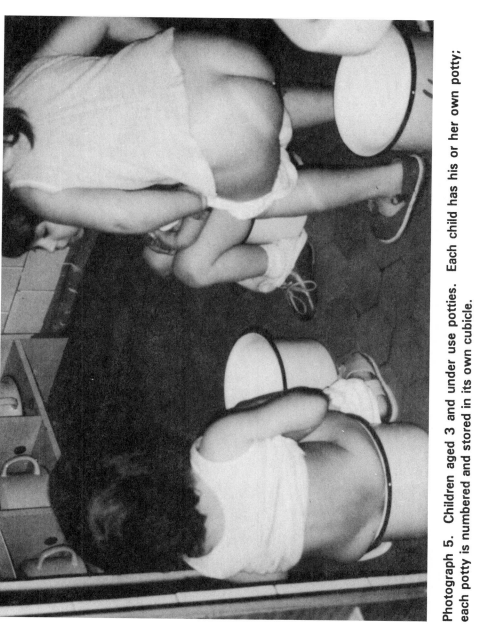

Photograph 5.   Children aged 3 and under use potties.   Each child has his or her own potty; each potty is numbered and stored in its own cubicle.

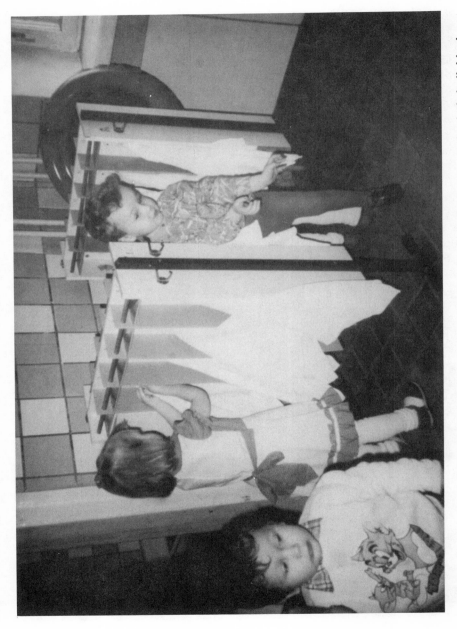

Photograph 6. After drying their hands, children hang their cloth towels back in their individual cubicles.

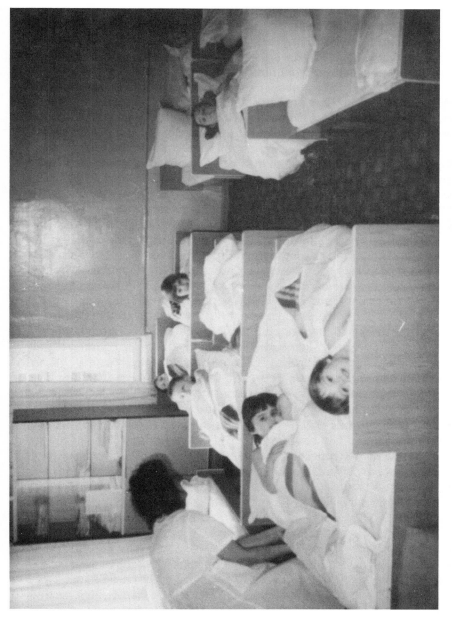

Photograph 7. A nanny tucks children in for nap time. Note the coziness of the beds and the head-to-foot arrangement.

expressed the hope that someday she would be able to do the same for her center.

The Music/Gym Room

All but the smallest center I visited contain one or two large rooms used for music lessons and physical education. In every case music rooms have a piano and about 30 child-sized chairs. When not in use, these chairs are placed along the walls, but during music lessons they are as likely as not arranged in rows near the piano. During holiday celebrations, when children perform well-rehearsed songs, dances, instrumental pieces, and games, these chairs are used by family members who come to watch. The walls in these rooms are typically dressed up with factory-produced pictures, woven cloths, and wooden decorations. Just as in the playrooms, there is no children's art on the walls.

In some centers, in addition to the music room there is a separate room for physical education. In other centers, the music and physical education rooms are one. Ladderlike climbing structures are standard equipment for physical education, as are beaded foot massagers and benches. Other items are brought out as needed.

The activities that take place in the indoor and outdoor spaces described above are outlined in some detail in the remainder of this book. The following chapter outlines typical daily routines. Later chapters focus on specific segments of the daily routine.

NOTE

1. Converting Centigrade to Fahrenheit, these temperatures translate to 5 degrees for 2-year-olds; -.4 degrees for 3- and 4-year-olds; and -4 degrees for 5- and 6-year-olds.

Chapter 6

The Daily Routine

Soviet pedagogical literature stresses the importance of instituting a daily routine for children that alternates active and quiet times, provides a variety of learning experiences, and ensures regular and nutritious meals, sound sleep, and fresh air. The benefits of following schedules that are suited to the child's natural rhythms of alertness and hunger are believed to be both physiological and psychological.

A correctly arranged schedule requires . . . (1) a definite length of time for lessons and work and rational alternation of these with periods of rest; (2) regular meals; (3) deep sleep; (4) enough time outside in the fresh air. The significance of the daily routine lies in the fact that it makes possible the normal functioning of the internal organs and physiological systems of the organism, permits a balanced, alert condition in the child, preserves the nervous system from exhaustion, creates favorable conditions for normal maturation, develops the ability to adapt to new situations, and permits stability in the face of negative influences. As a rule, children who have gotten used to an established schedule appropriate to their ages are well-disciplined, sociable, active; have even dispositions and good work habits; and rarely suffer from lack of appetite. (Bogina & Terekhova, 1987, p. 4)

Centers are open for children in daytime care from 7:00 a.m. to 7:00 p.m. Schedules for children in the age groups 2 to 3 years, 3 to 4 years, and 4 to 5 years differ mainly in terms of content and length (but not number) of activities and the length of the midday nap. For example, children in the 4- to 5-year-old groups have much the same schedule as children in the 3- to 4-year-old groups except that the older group's morning exercises and lessons last 5 minutes longer, lunch begins 15 minutes later, and naps are 10 minutes shorter.

Tatiana Bogina and Nina Terekhova (1987) recommend the following daily routine for groups with 2- and 3-year-olds. This schedule is for centers that, like those I visited, are open for children in day-only care from 7:00 a.m. to 7:00 p.m.

7:00 - 8:00   Children arrive. The nurse checks each child for fever and other signs of illness. Play and morning exercises.

8:00 - 8:30   Wash hands. Breakfast.

8:30 - 9:00   Play, preparation for lessons.

8:40 - 8:55   Lessons for Group I.

9:00 - 9:15   Lessons for Group II.

["Lessons" are focused, upbringer-led activities designed to teach skills or support emerging abilities. For the 15-minute lessons, the class is divided into two groups of seven or eight children. While the first small group has its lesson from 8:40 - 8:55, the children in the other small group play. During the second small group's lesson from 9:00 to 9:15, the first small group dresses to go outside.]

8:55 - 11:30   Outside time for Group I.

9:15 - 11:50   Outside time for Group II. [Each group goes outside right after its lesson. This arrangement minimizes waiting for Group I. It is also easier to help a smaller group put on winter outerwear.]

11:30 - 11:50   Group I returns inside [and takes off outdoor clothing].

11:50 - 12:10 Group II returns inside [and takes off outdoor clothing].

11:50 - 12:30 Wash hands. Lunch.

12:30 - 3:00 Preparation for naps. Sleep.

3:00 - 3:30 Gradual awakening, toileting, dressing, play.

3:30 - 4:00 Wash hands. Afternoon snack.

3:45 - 4:10 Play [for those who have finished their snacks].

4:10 - 4:25 Lessons for Group I.

4:25 - 4:40 Lessons for Group II.

[As in the morning, while the first small group is involved in the lesson, the other children engage in free play. While the second small group has its lesson, the first small group dresses to go outside.]

4:25 - 5:40 Dressing and outside time for Group I.

4:40 - 6:00 Dressing and outside time for Group II.

5:40 - 6:00 Group I returns inside [and removes outdoor clothing].

6:00 - 6:20 Group II returns inside [and removes outdoor clothing].

6:20 - 6:45 Wash hands. Dinner.

6:45 - 7:00 Play. Center closes. (pp. 9-10)

It is important to note that upbringers and children are not pressured to follow schedules exactly to the minute. While there was a close match between the recommended schedule and reality, particularly in the order of events, there was some flexibility in the exact timing of transitions from one part of the daily routine to the next.

Photograph 8. An upbringer leads children in morning exercises. They are pretending to be airplanes coming in for a landing.

With only one upbringer for 15 to 20 children, one might wonder how children are split into two smaller groups for lessons and the dressing and undressing routines associated with outside times. The answer is that these are times when nannies help. While Small Group I is having its lesson with the upbringer, the nanny watches Small Group II at free play. Then, while Small Group II is having its lesson, the nanny helps the children in Small Group I dress to go outside. At this point she either takes them out and stays with them until the upbringer and Small Group II come out, or she helps the children in Small Group II dress and takes them out. (In the latter case the upbringer would have gone out with Small Group I immediately after she finished her lesson with Small Group II.) Nannies do not stay outside for the duration of outside time. When it is time for Small Group I to return inside, the nanny comes outside to lead them in and help them undress.

The routine is simpler for the groups of 3- to 4- and 4- to 5-year-olds because these children are not divided into two groups for lessons and dressing/undressing. The group as a whole participates in lessons; dressing and undressing is also undertaken with all 20 children simultaneously. The nanny helps the upbringer in the dressing room but not with lessons.

What follows is the daily schedule for 3- and 4-year-olds as related to me by two directors of round-the-clock centers. Most of the children in these centers are picked up every night, but a few (up to 10) stay for the night. The schedule of these centers differs from that shown in Bogina and Terekhova's manual mainly in that lessons are 20 to 30 minutes long rather than only 15. As in the case of the schedule for 2- and 3-year-olds, for the sake of simplicity I have given what appear to be exact times. In actuality, however, directors spoke in more flexible terms. For example, I was told that morning exercises last until "about" 8:20 or 8:25.

7:00 - 8:10   Children arrive and are checked by the nurse. Play.

8:10 - 8:20   Morning exercises.

8:20 - 8:30   Wash hands for breakfast.

8:30 - 9:00   Breakfast. Play for those who finish before 9:00.

9:00 - 9:30   Lessons.

9:30 - 11:30   Dress to go outside; outside time.

11:30 - 12:00   Return inside; remove outdoor clothing; wash hands for lunch.

12:00 - 12:30   Lunch.

12:30 - 3:00   Preparation for naps; sleep.

3:00 - 3:30   Children awake and dress. Play.

3:30 - 4:00   Afternoon snack followed by play.

4:00 - 4:20   Lesson.

4:20 - 6:00   Dressing to go outside. Outside time.

6:00 - 7:00   Return inside. Take off outdoor clothing. Play.

7:00 - 7:30   Dinner.

7:30 - 9:00   Children who spend the night at the center watch a television show called "Good Night," engage in free play, and prepare for bed. All are in bed by 9:00.

In the past, parents were admonished not to bring children later than 8:00 a.m.; it was considered essential that children participate in all structured activities. Several directors told me that this rule had recently been relaxed and that now parents are encouraged but not required to bring children by 8:30 or 9:00, in time for lessons. I had some evidence that such flexibility is not the case in all centers. One day I arranged with an elderly woman to take a boat ride on the Moscow River. We met at about 11:00 a.m. She arrived with her granddaughter, Dasha, aged 4. Dasha's mother had allowed her to sleep late that morning. "It is so unpleasant to bring a child late, they give you such disapproving looks, we just decided to call and say that Dasha isn't coming at all today," she explained.

At the same time, it was clear to me that while the sequence of daily events is closely followed, there is flexibility in exact timing; upbringers may take into account the weather and the mood of the group that day. Bogina and Terekhova (1987) assure upbringers that it is all right, for example, to shorten indoor lessons on days when the weather is good so that more time can be spent outdoors and, in contrast, to assign more time to indoor lessons and play when the weather is inclement. Accordingly, one frigid afternoon I looked at my watch and noticed that children were dressing to go outside 20 minutes later than the schedule would have predicted. No one seemed perturbed about it.

Flexibility is also shown in the fact that schedules are a little different from center to center and from winter to summer. In the summer there is only one lesson per day, and more time is spent outdoors. On a related note, Bogina and Terekhova (1987) advise upbringers working in segregated round-the-clock groups to take advantage of the increased time they have available for all center activities. They suggest more flexibility for these groups, such as, for example, moving some of the morning lesson time to the afternoon so that more time in the morning can be spent outside.

Most children in daytime care have gone home by about 6:00. On Fridays, I discovered, a goodly number go home much earlier, especially in the spring, when parents take a few hours off from work to leave early for a weekend in the countryside. This trip is not all for pleasure. Nowadays many families have small plots of land near Moscow where they plant vegetables and berries to eat during the coming fall and winter.

On a related note, though directors told me that night work by parents, and consequently the demand for round-the-clock care, had diminished in recent years, many parents had started picking their children up later in the evening than they used to. Why? Because food shortages had made it more difficult to feed children at home. Parents were delaying their arrival until 7:00 or even 7:30 in the evening, so that children would be fed dinner at the center. Also more children were being left at the center for an occasional night. Perhaps parents were standing in line in stores late after work.

Interestingly, one director, chuckling, commented that not infrequently children ask to be left at the center overnight, thinking that it will be fun. I sensed that she was proud to have a program that was so attractive to children. "How do the parents react?" I asked, wondering if their feelings were hurt. "Oh, they are delighted. They get a free evening!" she replied, smiling. Looking back on this conversation, I wonder if this is an aspect of center care that parents will sorely miss in a capitalist economy. It is unlikely that many centers will be able to provide overnight care without the government subsidies of the Soviet era.

Chapter 7

Indoor Play

After they have passed the morning health check and put their outerwear in their closets, children arriving at the center before 8:00 a.m. proceed to the classroom for indoor play (*igra*). During *igra* children may choose the area of the playroom in which they will play, the materials they will use, and the peers with whom they will interact. They may play individually or in small groups, as they prefer.

One early morning I observed a busy room of 2- and 3-year-olds. Four boys rode around on riding toys. Two boys and a girl pretended to cook and eat in the housekeeping area. A boy and a girl strolled with doll carriages. Two girls worked on inserting pegs in a pegboard; two others drew with colored pencils. One girl looked at books. A boy and a girl built with blocks. A girl did somersaults on the housekeeping area rug. Occasionally, a child would run across the playroom. At one point a boy banged loudly on a drum. No one complained about the running or the noise.

Sometimes, especially later in the day when indoor play times are very short, the upbringer might invite children to play a whole-group circle game. A favorite involves having the children stand in a circle around the upbringer, a small flag (or handkerchief or rattle) on the floor in front of each child. As the upbringer approaches a given child, that child must quickly snatch the flag off the floor before the upbringer can get it. The first child to "lose" to the upbringer takes the upbringer's place in the middle of the circle. The game is then repeated with the child who is "it" trying to nab a flag. And so on. Photograph 9 was taken during one of these games.

Photograph 9. In a favorite circle game, children prepare to snatch their flags off the floor before the upbringer beats them to it.

Children are not forced to participate in circle games if they do not want to. The only real requirements for children during indoor play times are that they not hurt one another and that they put toys away after they have finished using them.

To the casual observer, *igra* thus looks much like a combination of indoor free play and circle time in the American preschool. It is not quite the same, however. First, except for children who come very early or stay very late, and except on very rainy or very cold days, there is not much time for *igra*. The reader may recall from the previous chapter that especially for children over the age of three, indoor play times between breakfast and dinner are short, 15 to 20 minutes in length. They seem designed mainly to help smooth transitions; children who are waiting for, or who have finished, an upbringer-led activity or a meal have only a few minutes to play independently until it is time for the next scheduled activity.

As will become clear from the descriptions to follow, *igra* also differs from American free play times in the degree and kind of adult involvement. With only one upbringer for 15 or 20 children, upbringer participation in children's play is necessarily limited. However, when the upbringer does get involved in play, she is likely to be considerably more directive than the American teacher.

These differences do not signify that play is viewed as unimportant by Russian early childhood educators. Far from it. Rather they see more need than Americans do to direct play, to enrich it, even to teach it. As for the amount of time available for indoor free play, it is limited largely because outdoor play takes precedence. Large blocks of outside time are considered essential for children's health. Moreover, much of the time spent outside is in fact devoted to free play (see Chapter 10).

WHY PLAY IS VALUED

Russian educators strongly believe that play is vital for children's social, emotional, and cognitive development. The early childhood literature credits Soviet psychologists such as Lev Vygotsky, Alexei Leontiev, Danil El'konin, and Alexander Zaporozhets, with demonstrating that young children's learning and development require active involvement with materials and people (e.g., Zvorigina, 1988).

Manuals for upbringers explain that play provides opportunities for the concrete, sensory experiences that young children need in order to understand the world around them. The upbringer is taught that young children are most receptive to learning during play because it is then that they are happiest and most fully engaged. For these reasons, play is viewed as a vehicle for developing a long list of cognitive skills and positive social-emotional attributes: persistence, industriousness, independence, initiative, creativity, representation, simple mathematics, language fluency, memory, fairness, sensitivity, responsiveness, and respect for adult work roles. Upbringers are made aware that during play, children can learn new information and skills or practice and extend what they have already learned.

RECOMMENDATIONS FOR PRACTICE FROM EARLY CHILDHOOD BOOKS

The developmental principles taught upbringers thus sound much like those one would expect to encounter in an American publication on child development. Also similar is the emphasis put on creating a warm, approving atmosphere in which children's individuality and initiative are respected and where enjoyable hands-on activities are readily available (e.g., Bondarenko & Voronova, 1986).

The differences are in some of the implications for practice. The American early childhood teacher would probably think that Soviet and Russian teaching manuals encourage adults to be too intrusively involved in children's play. It is true that though words such as *independence* and *initiative* figure prominently in these books, upbringers are advised that they should actively guide play, particularly when children are very young or when a new toy or activity is introduced. For example, upbringers of 2- and 3-year-olds are told that because children of this age have short attention spans, scant knowledge of the uses of various materials, and limited ability to engage in sustained play with peers, an adult must initiate and guide much of their play, working to maintain their interest in one activity so that flitting from toy to toy is reduced.

How does the upbringer do this? She is to capitalize on the fact that children of this age enjoy imitating adults. When children are playing with manipulatives or other "didactic" materials, the upbringer is to take the role of partner, arbitrator, evaluator. She is to explain how materials are to be used, help children play together.

To enrich dramatic play, the upbringer is to use literature, photographs, puppet shows, and field trips that acquaint children with adult work roles; she should point out the work that nannies and other center staff do and explain how important it is; she should enter role play to model how various workers do their jobs. During role play, she is advised to assign roles (keeping in mind children's individual interests and abilities) and to explain to each child what s/he should do. She is to demonstrate to children how to incorporate ready-made toys into role play and how to make additional props out of blocks, paper, and clay. She is to use clarifying comments, questions, and suggestions to motivate children to extend their play.

An emotional climate of enthusiasm, warmth, and approval is to be created. The upbringer is told to express excitement when playing with or teaching children, to choose materials and tasks that allow children to be successful, and to praise them for their efforts. To bolster self-confidence and to draw children into cooperative group play, the upbringer is advised to call attention to the positive characteristics of each child.

When children fight over toys, instead of reprimanding or punishing them, the upbringer is to redirect their attention or resolve their conflicts within a dramatic play theme. For example, if two children want to feed the same doll, she might point out that there is another hungry doll: "Look, Lena, this doll also wants to eat." Or she may separate the two children by giving them different roles, "Tania, you can feed the baby. Olia, the baby's bed is so messy. Here, you can help straighten it out" (Bondarenko & Voronova, 1986, pp. 59-60).

An example quoted from a supplement to the *Program for Upbringing and Teaching in the Preschool* gives the flavor of these recommendations:

> Before Katia turned 3, her hair had been cut at home, but for the holiday her mother took her to a beauty salon. The next day, in preschool, Katia decided to cut the hair of the dolls, teddy bears, and toy rabbits. She grabbed the toys from her friends, set the toys in front of the mirror, took out a comb, and, as she worked, repeated, "Snip, snip, snip, you've had a haircut; you're all pretty. And now pst, pst, pst, how you smell of perfume . . . that's all, go home." Then she threw the toys on the floor and went off to build a house. The upbringer, knowing that other children had attempted to play beauty salon too, decided to support this activity. "Katia, you're a hairdresser, right? Then why did you stop cutting hair? Look, Stepan (the rabbit) came to you in the beauty salon, and so did White Whiskers (the hare), and Zoia's braids are messy. Such a disheveled girl! Let's work

together. Here's your place: here's the table, mirror, razor, comb, cologne, scissors. And here's my set; I have everything too. So, who's next? Oh, Vova came with Misha the teddy bear! Hello, Vova! How would you like me to cut your child's hair? Oh, this way; I see. Sit here on this chair and put Misha in front of the mirror. We have Katia here, an excellent hairdresser. She cuts beautifully. And who else will come for a haircut? Probably Lena. Her daughter Lialia needs her hair braided and arranged around her cute little head. There! Pretty, yes?" Gradually the children got involved in this scene; they brought dolls and stuffed animals and sat waiting for their turn at the beauty shop. (Bondarenko & Voronova, 1986, pp. 60-61)

Here we see several of the recommendations for upbringers of 2- and 3-year-olds put into practice. Building on a child-initiated theme, the upbringer has managed to model what a worker (in this case a hairdresser) does and has shown children how to use the required equipment (comb, etc.). She has helped Katia play with more focus and has drawn in other children by making the activity seem interesting and by praising Katia for her involvement. As might be inferred from the monologue, she has not criticized Katia for grabbing toys or dropping things, but rather has enticed her back by her own enthusiasm for an activity that she knows has personal meaning for the child.

Recommendations are somewhat different for upbringers working with older children. By 4 and 5 years of age, children's social skills with peers improve; they know more about adult roles, enjoy dramatizing stories from literature and television, and are better able to initiate and sustain play. Accordingly, the upbringer is expected to allow them a somewhat greater role in initiating and directing their own play themes. At the same time, because it is understood that at this age children's desire to play with peers is often greater than their ability to do so peacefully, the upbringer is to remember to stay involved.

The upbringer is to try to find a way to satisfy the desires of all of the children participating in a given activity. Bondarenko and Voronova (1986) describe a dramatic play scene. The children were playing "hospital." The activity started to fall apart when all four decided they wanted to be the doctor. The upbringer intervened, describing various medical specializations and suggesting to one child that he could be a general practice doctor, to another that he could be a dentist, to another that she could be a veterinarian, and so on. This example is presented to show how an upbringer can use her influence to help children play together cooperatively within a sustained theme while at the same time teaching them about adult work roles. "The pedagogue . . . may take on the main, leading role or be one of the rank and file members, but in any case she must direct children's activity, guiding their initiative and creativity" (p. 67).

Bondarenko and Voronova (1986) explain that as children get closer to school age, 6 and 7 years of age, it is preferable to guide play "carefully, tactfully," so that the children's initiative and creativity are not stifled and children barely notice the upbringer's influence. An important part of the upbringer's role is to continue to introduce children to literary figures and stories and to deepen their understanding of and respect for the complexity of adult work. By this age, competition can also be used to motivate children.

INDOOR PLAY IN ACTUAL PRACTICE

I observed extended indoor free play times on a number of occasions when it was either raining or too cold to stay outside the prescribed 1 1/2 to 2 hours. Below I briefly describe 10 scenes; in each case I have focused on upbringer-child interaction.

Scene 1: During afternoon indoor play time, an upbringer working with 2-year-olds suggested that they build a road and a house from blocks. She sat down on the floor and started building while her charges watched. Gradually, the children started to join in. At first they simply handed her blocks, but after a while they too started to add blocks to the road. At this point the upbringer sat back and watched. "Oh, what a pretty road!" she exclaimed.

Scene 2: Several 4-year-old children wearing handmade red cloth hats with white circles over the ears (space helmets) built a rocket out of blocks. The rocket reached to their shoulders. The upbringer came by, explained that the rocket was unstable because it was too tall, and showed them how to make it shorter and wider. She then suggested that they build a garage for the rocket and showed them how to do it. Later, after the children had worked on the garage, she exclaimed how pretty it was.

Scene 3: A child was building a structure out of blocks. It had no roof. The upbringer asked him what might happen to a building with no roof. He started adding one.

Scene 4: A group of 3-year-olds decided to play doctor. One girl called the hospital on the telephone. The upbringer came over to tell her what to tell the doctor. Then she looked for a doctor's robe. First she found one that was for a barber; that one would not do. Finally she found the right one. After tying the robe on the "doctor," she directed: "Turn her [the doll] around. Listen to her breathing. Take her temperature." The child put a thermometer to the doll's mouth. The upbringer continued, "Give her this medicine so she will feel better." The "doctor" did as she was told. "Good for you!" the upbringer praised her. Other children crowded around, but only the child who was the doctor was allowed to use the medical equipment. "Now here's another sick doll. Open your case. Good. Listen to her cute little chest. Apply cupping glasses to her. You're the mother. Nowadays mothers have to be able to do everything." (A reference to the recent decline in medical care.) After the children were finished playing doctor, the upbringer carefully hung the costumes back up on a hanger. Throughout the episode her voice and facial expressions suggested great enjoyment and emotional involvement.

Scene 5: Another upbringer also directed a medical play episode. This time I heard more questioning of the children, but the upbringer seemed to have particular right answers in mind. She had gone over to a corner in which several children had gathered around a doll. They were pretending that the doll was sick and were deciding what to do. The upbringer stepped in, picked up the receiver of a toy telephone and urgently "called" a doctor. After hanging up, she directed one child to take the doll's temperature. The child reported that the patient had a fever.

UPBRINGER (acting worried): "He has a fever? What do we need to do?"
CHILD: "Give him medicine. This [a stacking toy] will be the medicine." The child fed the doll some medicine.
UPBRINGER: "Good. Now what else?"
CHILD: "Give him a shot."
UPBRINGER: "And what should we do with the prescription the doctor gave us?" [After hearing no answer to her question, the upbringer continued] "We need to go to the drugstore."

Photograph 10 was taken during this episode.

Scene 6: A child complained that her doll wouldn't go to sleep.

UPBRINGER: "Maybe first she needs to go outside to play."
CHILD: "She'll sleep first, then go out."

UPBRINGER: "Fine."

Scene 7: Two children were playing doctor. The "patient" lay down and pulled up her dress so the "doctor" could examine her. The upbringer came over and told her to pull her dress down. "The way you're lying isn't pretty."

Scene 8: An upbringer sat on a chair, reading to three children while they waited for lunch. They stood by her, listening intently.

Scene 9: A 4-year-old boy had been pretending to be a cosmonaut but had lost interest. He looked bored and glum. The upbringer approached, "What, my golden one, are you tired?" She offered him a truck. He shook his head. "What, my good one, what would you like to do? Would you like to draw?" The boy again shook his head. Smiling, her arm around him and looking genuinely concerned, the upbringer offered him a pull toy. Again he refused. Finally the upbringer succeeded in gaining his interest when she suggested they build a road together out of blocks so that he could drive cars on it.

Scene 10: It was right after afternoon snack time in a classroom of 4-year-olds. The children were engaged in noisy indoor free play. The 68-year-old nanny came in for a minute to get the dirty snack dishes. Proudly, she pointed out to me a boy who could already read and do simple arithmetic. Picking up on the mood, a girl showed off, reciting a long poem by heart. Her friend followed with another recitation. Meanwhile, the upbringer watched but did not interact with children except to respond to conflicts. After a while, she became immersed in setting up the tables for the lesson she was to teach in a few minutes.

What can we make of these vignettes? They are illustrative of some of the recommendations described above. First, it is clear that upbringers believe that play is important. In almost all of the scenes, play was encouraged both through the provision of materials and through modeling and suggestions regarding their use.

Moreover, upbringers saw it as appropriate to take on a lead role in developing and directing children's play, to show children what to do and how to do it. Scenes 1, 2, 3, 4, 5, and 9 are indicative. In Scene 1, the upbringer gave 2-year-olds a direct suggestion about what they might do and then began the activity for them, gradually backing off as children became involved. The children in Scene 2 were older. They themselves had started building. The upbringer explained what was wrong with their block structure, then

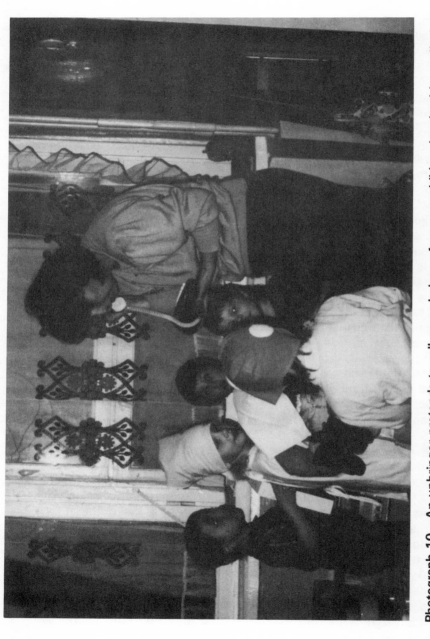

Photograph 10. An upbringer pretends to call an ambulance for some children involved in medical play. The child with the tall white cap is the "doctor"; the nurse is next to her, wearing a white kerchief. The child in the foreground with the cap with circles on it is a "cosmonaut" who moved over from another area to watch.

proceeded to take over, showing exactly how to rebuild and expand. In Scene 3, though the upbringer asked an open question, she implied that the structure the children had made was lacking a necessary element, that it must have a roof to be satisfactory.

Similar comments can be made about the two medical play scenes (4 and 5). In both, the upbringer picked up on a role play activity the children were just initiating and enthusiastically took the lead role. In Scene 4, the children were told exactly what to do and say; even the doctor's robe had to be just right. In Scene 5, the children had more flexibility (e.g., a stacking toy could be used to represent medicine), but still it was the upbringer, and not the children, who was in charge.

In Scene 9 we again see the responsibility the upbringer feels for helping children become involved in play. At the same time, it is important to note that the child in this episode felt free to turn down the upbringer's suggestions. The same can be said about Scene 6. In both cases children were not afraid to say no to their upbringers. In Scene 6, the upbringer was willing to accept the child's plan even when it contradicted her own. In Scene 9, the upbringer continued brainstorming until she hit upon an idea the child liked.

Scenes 4, 5, and 9 are important also because they illustrate the genuine warmth that many upbringers display toward their charges. This is in accord with professional recommendations on maintaining a climate of warmth, good cheer, and concern for each child. Upbringers are encouraged to be emotionally expressive, to convey affection and enthusiasm for the children they work with and the activities they engage in.

It might be noted that in 6 of the 10 vignettes, children were praised. The Russian early childhood literature contends that praise motivates not only the child being praised, but also the other children who hear it (e.g., Peterina, 1986). In Scenes 1, 2, 4, and 5, the upbringer's praise was aimed at making the children feel successful and motivating them to want to continue to involve themselves in the kinds of activities they were engaged in at the time. Since children were praised after following through on upbringers' suggestions, one might guess that a by-product might be children's willingness to accept adult leadership in matters of play. In Scene 10, the effect of the nanny's praise of one child on the behavior of another is illustrative of one of the intended consequences of praise. The girl who recited poetry had heard a boy being praised for his abilities and wanted to do something that would garner her similar approval. Certainly in these classrooms the praise given children also conveyed warmth. This was particularly apparent in Scene 9, when the upbringer called a child "my good boy" as she attempted to cheer him up.

Upbringers' belief in the importance of aesthetic qualities was reflected in three scenes. In Scenes 1 and 2 children were praised for the attractiveness of their products. In Scene 7 we see that not only should children's products be pretty, but also the children themselves. Because immodesty is not "pretty," children are to keep their clothes in place even when it interferes with the realism of their dramatic play.

Scene 8 is noteworthy because it shows an upbringer taking a few minutes to read to a very small group of children. Because of the large ratio of adults to children, this cannot happen as often as many educators would like. In fact, as shown in Scene 10, the response of some upbringers is to withdraw into passive watching. This is certainly not the preferred style. Nor, in the centers in which I observed, was it the norm.

PUTTING THINGS AWAY

During indoor play times, children must neatly put away materials or toys before changing to a different activity and before going home. (Occasionally there are exceptions—when, for example, children have been working on a block structure and are allowed to leave it standing while they go outside.) Children are encouraged to help one another with cleanup and are praised for doing so. Of course, being children, they do not always remember on their own. Upbringers and nannies do some tidying up themselves, but the preferred method of keeping the room neat is to make the children responsible for putting away the items they have used.

Sometimes the reminders are simple and direct. Some examples from my notes: "Put the cars away. We're going to draw now. Put the toys away. Everything in its place." Or "Put away the toys. Time to wash your cute little hands." One upbringer nodded to a boy who was not complying with a request to clean up. Pointing to a toy, she repeated herself in a quiet, calm voice. This time he listened. "Good for you!" the upbringer praised him when he had finished. On another occasion, an upbringer waiting to start an afternoon lesson remarked to a 4-year-old who was slowly putting away his toys, "Andriusha, I am waiting for you." These words were sufficient; he cleaned up.

Sometimes a favorite activity is used as a carrot. One day I was observing in a classroom of 2-year-olds. It was close to lunchtime. The upbringer told them it was time to put away their blocks and cars, but they continued to play. The upbringer enticed them with a bargain. After they had put the toys away "so the room will look pretty," they could play "rabbit." The bait worked; the children quickly cleaned up. "Oi! How nicely you cute little children have put the cars away so they won't be in our way. You yourselves are cute little rabbits!" enthused the upbringer. Then she led the promised game; the children pretended to be baby rabbits hopping away from a mean wolf. When it was time to wash hands, the children did not want to stop playing. The upbringer assured them that they could play again in the afternoon.

Many times requests to clean up were couched in language that invited children to see cleaning up as just another part of play. Early childhood manuals encourage the use of this technique (e.g., Kutsakova & Pushnina, 1986). My observation notes contain many examples. Often I heard upbringers tell children to "park" their riding toys in the "garage." The garage was simply a designated area by one wall. One creative upbringer suggested that the children make an incline, so that they could roll the toy cars to their assigned places. After she had made the incline, using three blocks, and demonstrated how it could be used, the children happily rolled their cars to the "parking lot." After all the cars had been parked, they put the blocks away too.

Sometimes children are induced to clean up to please the toys that need to be put away. One boy had dropped a toy horse on the floor. "Sasha, your horse is crying. It fell. Put it away." A doll was lying face down on the floor. "Oi! Mashka, your daughter is crying. She hurt her nose. Quick, put her in bed!" A blow-up crocodile that I had given one classroom was left out on the floor. The upbringer asked the children where they should keep it after they had played with it. One child suggested, "Here in this cabinet." The upbringer pointed out that "it'll be too tight. His tail will get hurt. Let's put him on this shelf so he'll be more comfortable."

In this chapter I have attempted to give the flavor of indoor play times. The closest equivalent in the American preschool is "free play," yet the amount of control exercised by teachers is quite different in the two cultures. Some of the younger upbringers mentioned to me that they feel tension between the requirement that they direct play and the requirement that they not squelch children's independence and initiative. Recently, Boguslavskaia and

Smirnova (1991) charged that not only is free play accorded insufficient time but that too many educators view it as just another chance to reinforce the knowledge gained during lessons. They argue that children should be presented with more opportunities to choose their own play themes at their preferred levels of complexity. Perhaps democratization in the society as a whole will bring with it more time and more respect for children's self-initiated play.

Chapter 8

Lessons: General Features

During the school year, from September to June, center schedules call for two 15- to 20-minute lessons each day, one in the morning after breakfast and one in the afternoon after snack time. The purpose of lessons is to systematically teach children particular skills and abilities.

For children aged 2 to 4, the *Program* recommends lessons in five main areas: (a) three each week in art—drawing, sculpture, construction, appliqué; (b) two each week in literature, science, or social studies; (c) one each week in "elementary mathematical concepts"—number, spatial and temporal concepts, and classification; (d) two each week in music; and (e) three each week in physical education—two during regular lesson Times and one during outside time. During the summer months there is only one lesson each day, and none in art, literature, science, social studies, or mathematics. Only music and physical education lessons continue year-round. Weather permitting, these are held outside.

In some ways lessons are similar to one another regardless of content area. This chapter describes these common features. Details specific to lessons in the different content areas are presented in Chapter 9.

Typically, the regular classroom upbringer conducts all lessons except music lessons, which are taught by specialists. In groups with children aged 2 and 3, half the class participates at a time. The nanny watches the other children engage in free play or, if they have just had their lesson, she helps them dress to go outside. In rooms with children aged 4 and older, the upbringer works with the entire class at the same time.

Lessons have three stages: preparation, implementation, and evaluation.

PREPARATION

Because of limited resources, the behind-the-scenes work the upbringer must do to prepare materials may be quite time-consuming by American standards. For example, one upbringer spent time painting 15 sheets of paper blue the day before a lesson on drawing fish. She lacked blue construction paper and wanted the children to have water for their fish.

But preparation for a lesson involves much more than preparing materials and planning the instructional process. It also involves preparing children. This means introducing the lesson in such a way that children are motivated to participate. This is especially important because many lessons require children to learn and practice skills that are not interesting in their own right. An example is drawing many small circles on a page.

To capture children's interest, the upbringer might read or tell a story that embeds the activity in a dramatic play theme. For example, if the lesson plan does call for children to practice drawing many small circles, she might read them a story about thirsty flowers, then ask them to help the flowers by drawing some "rain." She would probably follow her request by drawing some circles herself, explaining as she does it, "First I make one little circle of rain, then another one right next to it, then another." Her model is left on an easel at the front of the room for children to copy. (Turn back to Photograph 4 in Chapter 5 for an example. The easel in that picture holds the upbringers' model paintings of the sun. Children could refer to them as they worked.)

Upbringers are to capitalize on the fact that young children are captivated by materials and events that are bright and lively, or new and surprising. The use of "surprises" is very much encouraged, particularly for the youngest children (Bondarenko & Voronova, 1986). In their book on art activities, Tatiana Doronova and Sophia Yakobson (1992) suggest that upbringers camouflage lessons on drawing short vertical lines in dramatic play episodes that begin with unexpected telephone calls. In one of their suggested scenarios, at the start of the lesson the upbringer makes the sound of a telephone ringing even as she pretends to be surprised and excited to hear it. "Oh, hello, mother rabbit!" she exclaims into the receiver. Then, after many words of sympathy, she ends the "conversation" with the rabbit by telling her not to worry, that the children in her room will surely come to her aid. Hanging up, she explains to the children that the mother rabbit is very upset because some mice have ruined the field where she lives. Now there is hardly any grass for her babies eat and play in. All is not lost, though, the upbringer tells the children; they can draw some grass (i.e., short green vertical lines) to give to the rabbit family. The lesson now begins; the assignment–to fill a page with short green vertical lines.

Another frequently used type of surprise is an unexpected visit from a doll or stuffed animal. Typically, there is a knock at a door; when the upbringer opens it, she discovers behind it a favorite doll or stuffed animal who just decided to drop by with some materials for the children to use. For example, one day I watched as Burratino (a story character resembling our Pinnochio) brought some geometric shapes to the playroom. He wanted to see if the children could put them together. In this case the nanny was the one doing the knocking, but in classrooms without nannies, upbringers hide the materials beforehand and then orchestrate the "surprise" themselves.

IMPLEMENTATION

Upbringers can find sample activities in the *Program* and in supplementary manuals. As mentioned in Chapter 2, by the late 1980s upbringers were no longer required to follow the *Program* to the letter. Nonetheless the expectations for children listed in the *Program* were still subscribed to at the time of my visit.

The ideal lesson exposes children to concepts or techniques in their "zone of proximal development" (Bogina & Terekhova, 1987; Bondarenko & Voronova, 1986). This "zone," first conceptualized by the Soviet psychologist Vygotsky and now of considerable interest in the West, is a theoretical construct describing skills just beyond a child's present capabilities but to which s/he can be led through interaction with a more advanced individual (typically an adult or older child). Activities that require children to perform in this zone are motivating because they are challenging, but not so hard that the child cannot be successful (Vygotsky, 1978). To stay in this zone, lessons are to contain some repetition of skills or concepts introduced in previous lessons plus the teaching of slightly new ones. For example, after several lessons on drawing short vertical lines, children are asked to draw short horizontal lines (Doronova & Yakobson, 1992). Lessons that are too hard for a given developmental level are avoided because children will lose interest or, worse yet, become "nervous and sickly" (Bogina &

Terekhova, 1987, p. 52).   When the upbringer sees that children have tired of a lesson, she is to bring it to a close. Returning to the example above, the upbringer might pick up a toy stuffed rabbit and announce that the mother rabbit has come for the grass the children have drawn for her.   The mother rabbit thanks the children and takes their drawings away with her.

American early childhood specialists tend to believe that young children should be given maximum freedom to explore various media and their own abilities. Technique can wait; teaching it early will dampen motivation and creativity (e.g., Edwards & Nabors, 1993). Not so Russian educators. They believe technique should be taught first. Later, as one upbringer explained to me, children can be allowed freedom to do as they wish. By then they will know the fundamental skills and will incorporate them in their personal creations.   Doronova and Yakobson support this upbringer: "So that a small child can learn to draw, he must have control over the main movements needed to produce shapes (he must be able to make certain lines, circular forms, etc.).   This process demands from the young child systematically organized practice" (1992, p. 15). Accordingly, the first two lessons in their program for 2- and 3-year-olds involve teaching them how to hold pencils and paint brushes correctly and how to draw short vertical lines. Subsequent lessons focus on drawing short lines going in other directions. Only toward the end of the year is the upbringer to encourage children to be creative in their artwork.

A related belief is that children cannot on their own come to the realizations and skills being taught.   It is not enough to make materials available to children; it is also necessary to engage them in didactic interchanges and adult-directed sensory experiences with these materials. Without adult guidance, children cannot reach their full potential, and their perceptions will be impoverished. Note, for example, the following caution from a manual on play: "The conscious, goal-directed perception of color is not an inborn trait. Only adults can help children see the world of colors, catch all the diversity in color tones, and form stable visual images of color" (Boguslavskaia & Smirnova, 1991, pp. 76-77).   Another manual contains an answer to those who would ask why representation needs to be taught, when children naturally, of their own accord, engage in pretend play, drawing, and construction.   "Exactly because this happens spontaneously, without proper direction from adults, the level of intellectual abilities of different children is exceedingly different, the potential of every child is far from fully realized" (Venger, D'iachenko, Govorova, & Tsekhanskaia, 1989, p. 6).

Another feature of lessons is the prominent place given to the teaching of vocabulary. Vocabulary drill is characteristic of many lessons, not only those in language and literature. Many lessons, particularly those in "elementary mathematics," devote significant attention to children's learning of words for objects, characteristics of objects, and relations among objects. The reason for this is the belief that children's perception and learning are much enhanced when they can attach labels to stimuli and concepts. For example, an explanation accompanying directions for activities teaching color words notes: "The young child's color perception is elevated to a higher level if in everyday life he actively labels colors" (Boguslavskaia & Smirnova, 1991, p. 77).

It should be noted that a book published the same year challenges this notion:

Acquainting children with the different characteristics of objects, one should not insist on the memorization and use of their labels. The main thing is that the child should take the characteristics of objects into account when he acts on them. And it is not a tragedy if he calls a triangle "angle" or "roof." The adult, working with children, uses the names for forms and colors, but does not demand this of her charges. (Venger, Piliugina, & Venger, 1991, p. 6)

The exception, write the authors, concerns words for size (big, small). They contend that because the size of an object is always relative to other objects, this concept can be understood only if assimilated in verbal form. Even they, it thus appears, are not fully willing to dismiss the importance of correct labeling for concept development.

What happens if children will not or cannot perform as required? They are helped to do so. The style of helping would probably be called intrusive by American teachers. For example, Tatiana Doronova and Sophia Yakobson recommend that if the upbringer notices that a child is not drawing short lines as requested for a given lesson, she hold the child's arm and guide it.

Photograph 11 shows this happening. The upbringer had prepared these 2-year-olds for the lesson by showing them pictures and plastic models of fish and reciting a poem about them. The first instruction to the children was to "hold the brush correctly. Look at me. Hold it in your right hand the way I am." She walked around repositioning brushes and fingers of children who were holding their brushes incorrectly or in the left hand. (The one left-handed child was allowed to keep his in his left hand after the upbringer reminded herself out loud that he was a "leftie.") Next the upbringer drew a fish herself and held it up as an example. "My fish is yellow. Yours can be yellow or red. Now hold the corner of the paper with your left hand so it won't slip." The child in the photograph just sat looking at his paper; the upbringer came over and gently guided his arm so that fish were drawn. Upon the conclusion of the lesson, all of the children were praised ("All of you drew well.") even though, as would be expected for this age group, most of the fish were actually formless squiggles.

Recall that "play form" is often used at the beginning of lessons to motivate children to participate. It may also be used during the activity to encourage children to do better work. One play form tactic is for upbringers to speak through dolls. A doll offers suggestions to children about how they could improve their performance. This is viewed as less threatening and at the same time often more effective than if the upbringer were to directly correct children.

Another "play form" tactic is for the upbringer to speak directly to children about the shortcomings in their work but to couch the remonstrative words within the story theme used to introduce the lesson. For example, the upbringer might tell children who draw only a few blades of grass that the rabbits will be happier if the grass is thicker (this particular example is given in Doronova & Yakobson, 1992). I saw this strategy in action many times. During a lesson on drawing the sun, for example, I watched as the upbringer approached children who had drawn only a few rays. She shivered, "Oh! I am cold! Draw more rays! Rays warm the ground. Draw straight ones, like mine." As children complied, she thanked them, "Good for you! Smart boy [or girl]! Now I am warm."

The *Program* calls for respect for individual differences; recent books for upbringers also sound this note. For upbringers trained in the old school, this is not easy to achieve. For them, permitting a child to draw a sun along with the required fish, or permitting some suns to be yellow and some to be orange, some to have more rays than others, fulfills the demand to allow for individual differences. I saw signs, however, that freedom of expression was emerging in some classrooms.

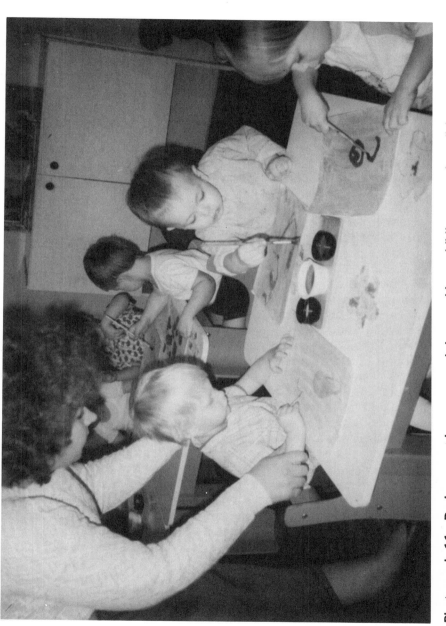

Photograph 11. During an art lesson, an upbringer guides a child's arm to draw fish.

It was interesting to see these signs, and also to detect tensions between the old and the new. One of my first days in Moscow I was escorted to a *yasli* by a researcher from the Institute for Preschool Education. She was trying to train upbringers to allow children more freedom in their art. We were in a classroom of 2½- to 3-year-olds. Small cups of yellow paint, red paint, and water, separate brushes for each color, blotting paper, and construction paper were neatly arranged on a table. The children were given a choice of color of construction paper and reminded to rinse their brushes in the water and press them on the blotting paper after they had used them. Having given these instructions, the upbringer asked them what they would like to paint. The researcher interceded, "Let them draw now; later they will tell us what they have drawn." The upbringer commented that one child is left-handed. "That's all right," the researcher assured her. (Twenty years ago left-handed children were trained to use their right hands; this is no longer the practice, but left-handed children are still pointed out as different.) "Draw whatever you like," she told the children.

After the children had finished painting, they were asked what they had drawn. One child, who had painted an oval shape with a lattice in the middle, said she had drawn a fish. Another said that the white spots he had made on his paper were rabbits. "Very pretty," he was complimented. Another was praised for not painting outside the lines of the shape she had made. When one girl remained silent after being asked what she had drawn, the researcher kept repeating "what is it?" until the girl finally murmured an answer that I could not hear. At an age when scribbling is the developmental norm (Brittain, 1979), children were nonetheless expected to be precise and to draw "something."

Another day I was in a classroom of 5-year-olds. The children had been given paper and colored pencils and were to draw their favorite animals. At first it seemed a typical old-style lesson with little room for children's creativity. The upbringer walked around the room checking on children as they drew. One child had decided to draw a cat but seemed stumped as to how to proceed. The upbringer advised her, "Cats have round heads, oval bodies, sharp little ears like triangles. What kind of tail?" As the child finished drawing according to these instructions, the upbringer praised her work, "Look how nice he is!" Another child was told to "draw some grass. Make it green." "Poor thinking," one girl was told; from the angle where I was sitting I couldn't see her drawing. One child was drawing a rooster. "Draw a comb," said the upbringer.

When the child said she didn't know how, the upbringer did it for her.

But then came the surprise—to me, at least. A boy who was sitting near me had muttered that he couldn't draw an animal. After a few minutes of looking into space, he had proceeded to draw an unrecognizable but artful creature. As the upbringer approached him, he looked worried. But when she looked at his paper, instead of criticizing his work, she exclaimed with apparent approval in her voice, "Well, you have your own kind of animal! A fantastical one, yes." After the upbringer had collected the papers, this boy, perhaps misunderstanding her tone, asked if he could have his back so he could cross out his animal, tear it up. "No, you shouldn't," the upbringer gently chided him. "I like your fantastical animal very much."

This child's reaction, combined with the "poor thinking" comment noted above, suggested to me that permission for creativity was either inconsistently applied or relatively new in this classroom. In another classroom, however, I watched as a young upbringer who was fresh out of the pedagogical institute conducted a sculpture lesson. As I observed, I thought how different her recent training must have been from that of her older colleagues.

The children in this room were 5 1/2 to 6 years old. The upbringer began the lesson with some remarks about the fact that flowers would soon be blooming (it was March). "What do we put cut flowers in?" she asked the children. "In vases," they replied. "Yes, and today we are going to make vases out of plasticine." She turned the children's attention to three vases on her desk. Pointing out that the vases were not identical, she explained that vases come in many different shapes, sizes, and colors. The children were invited to make their vases any way they wished. If they liked, they could also make branches with leaves and flowers. Each child was given a plate with some plasticine, a stylus, and a plastic square on which to work (so that the tables would not be dirtied). The only further instructions were reminders to sit "straight and pretty" and to roll and squeeze the plasticine to soften it. Some children also blew on it. Then they got to work, sculpting quietly and with great concentration. Photograph 12 shows the vases made during this lesson. No two look alike. Children who did not finish their vases by the end of the allotted time were assured that they could do so after nap time.

Photograph 12. This upbringer had instructed children to make vases anyway they wished. Here they gather around the finished vases for the evaluation.

EVALUATION

Lessons conclude with an evaluation of children's work. This assessment usually follows immediately after the lesson, but occasionally it is delayed until after outside time.

At the conclusion of music, large motor, and other lessons that do not result in products, upbringers make some comments about how well the children followed directions, helped one another, actively participated, and so on. Individual children's names may be used, or the upbringer may discuss the accomplishments of the group as a whole.

For the evaluation of performance during lessons resulting in visible products (e.g., art), all of the children's works are displayed, and the class (or, in the case of younger children, the subgroup) gathers around them. The upbringer shares her opinions, praising the group as a whole and singling out for special compliments those who were attentive, who worked neatly, who produced the most detailed or otherwise laudable result. Play form is recommended especially for very young children. For example, after a lesson on block building, the upbringer might exclaim, "My car is going to Olya's gates. How pretty her gates are! How evenly she placed the blocks!" (Kutsakova, 1986, p. 347)

Often children are also invited to speak. After one art lesson that I observed, the upbringer held up each picture and asked the "artist" to explain it. On other occasions, children were asked for their opinions about the work of their peers.

What is the purpose of these evaluations? One is to help the upbringer think through what she should do during subsequent lessons. But the direct consequences for children are of greater importance. "Children's work must be evaluated because this motivates them to improve. The analysis should be for the sake of education and upbringing and should not be perfunctory, as when the upbringer at the end of the lesson, addressing the children, simply says, 'Everyone worked well, everyone built attractively and neatly except Vova and Sasha'" (Kutsakova, 1990, p. 4). Evaluations at the end of lessons are thus primarily for the purpose of inspiring children to work hard and to behave themselves during future lessons. They are also thought to foster in children the inclination to be self-evaluative. This is why children may be asked to comment on their own work as well as on that of their peers.

The concluding evaluation is also used as an aid in aesthetic education. Boguslavskaia and Smirnova, for example, recommend that at the end of a lesson requiring 3- and 4-year-old children to make "rugs" by fitting together variously colored geometric shapes, the upbringer ask children to judge whose rug is prettiest. "This promotes not only visual perception of the forms, but also artistic taste" (1991, p. 107).

All of the Soviet and Russian early childhood texts that I have read strongly recommend that the upbringer's evaluative comments focus on the positive. Warning that this is not a time to shame children who do not do as well as others (recall her quotation above), Kutsakova writes that "every child must see that the upbringer cares about his work, that she took it in her hands, looked it over. Encouragement can take on various forms. It can be a friendly, affectionate word, a gesture, a silent squeeze of a child's hand. The preschooler will be delighted if sometimes he finds on his work, for instance, a happy, smiling sun drawn by the upbringer" (1990, p. 4). Bondarenko and Voronova (1986) suggest that the upbringer find something praiseworthy to say about each child's performance. "The upbringer notes who followed the rules, who helped his comrades, who was active, who was honest" (p. 77).

When criticism is warranted, Kutsakova suggests, the upbringer is wise to have a toy, not herself, make the complaint. For example, a teddy bear could point out to a child that his house would have been better had he not been fooling around during the lesson. Children are better able to accept this kind of play form critique. Older children are to be taught to tactfully and respectfully comment on each other's projects; they are to learn not to have hard feelings when others point out the shortcomings of their work or tell them how they might have done something differently.

Immediately after the evaluation, the upbringer is to say something about the next lesson so that the children will look forward to it. For example: "Today we played well. . . . Next time a 'magic bag' will come to us. We will guess what is in it" (Bondarenko & Voronova, 1986, p. 78).

Twenty years ago, when I first observed art lessons, upbringers would call on a child to come to the front of the room to comment on which drawings (or sculptures) s/he thought were best. Upbringers would then add their own evaluations. On this visit I saw nothing so heavy-handed, but the message was still clear that some children's works were better than others.

Two examples come to mind. In one case, a group of 3-year-olds had all drawn pictures of the sun. After they were finished, the upbringer exclaimed that she especially liked one child's sun, that in fact she liked it so much that she was going to draw a face in the middle of it. As she proceeded to do so, I thought to myself how different this was from what I would expect at home; trained American preschool teachers would likely think it an infringement on the child's work to change it in any way. Note, however, that the upbringer's action was very much in keeping with Kutsakova's quoted recommendation.

A second example involves the sculpture lesson described earlier. As children finished sculpting their vases, they placed them on a table to exhibit them. After almost everyone had completed the work and cleaned up, the upbringer had them gather around the exhibit (see Photograph 12). The children were asked which vases they liked best. "I like this one because it is pretty," said one. "I like that one because it is bright," said another. The comments continued: "I like the color of this one." "This one has pretty designs." "I like them all." The upbringer concluded the evaluation session with words meant to make children whose vases had not been complimented feel better: "We like all the vases very much. You children really tried hard."

The reader may be reminded of the "review" stage of the "plan-do-review" cycle of the Cognitively Oriented Curriculum of the High/Scope Educational Research Foundation in Ypsilanti, Michigan (Hohmann, Banet, & Weikart, 1979). There is a major difference, however. In the Cognitively Oriented Curriculum, the emphasis is on children reviewing their own work; in the Russian case, the child's work is assessed by others.

On my last day in Moscow, I met with several directors and curriculum specialists for a farewell get-together. They asked if I had any suggestions for them, any criticisms of their centers. I told them that I was uneasy with the evaluations that followed lessons, that I worried that some children might suffer from feelings of inadequacy when their work was not singled out as among the best. The words of praise directed to the entire group after a few children's work had won specific praise may be dismissed by children whose names aren't mentioned individually. One director agreed that perhaps I was right; some discussion followed that perhaps this practice needed to be rethought. The openness of these individuals to both positive and negative feedback was impressive, particularly against the backdrop of the wall that had existed only a few years before.

Chapter 9

Lessons: Content Area Specifics

The previous chapter described features that apply to lessons generally. This chapter reports on details specific to lessons in each of the five main instructional areas (art, language/the surrounding world, mathematical concepts, music, and physical education). The skills children are expected to acquire and the teaching methods particular to each content area are presented. The discussion draws from the Soviet/Russian early childhood literature and from my observations.

Recently there has been encouragement to develop lessons bridging the five areas (for example, having children use movement and song to express their feelings toward a piece of literature). The year before I visited, one of the centers sponsored by the Moscow city subway system had received a prize in recognition of its successes at this "combination method." Most of the lessons I observed, however, were distinctly focused in one content area.

Because I was interested in learning about Russian practice for children comparable in age to American preschoolers, I limited most of my observing to classrooms of children aged 2 to 4 years. Similarly, the information I have drawn from the literature concerns 2-, 3-, and 4-year-olds. Although some centers in Russia have mixed-age groupings, in all six centers in which I observed the children in each classroom were within a year of each other in age. Upbringers thus developed each lesson plan with only one age group in mind.

ART

Art lessons provide instruction in drawing, painting, sculpture, appliqué (pasting shapes and figures on paper), and construction (using blocks, paper, and natural materials such as sand, snow, and twigs). Each week children have one lesson in drawing and one in sculpture. Construction and appliqué alternate for the third weekly art lesson so that there are two lessons in each per month.

The information presented below on goals for art lessons are drawn from publications by A. A. Gribovskaia, T. N. Doronova, N. B. Khalezova, and T. V. Chernik (1986), by Liudmila Kutsakova (1986), and by A. A. Gribovskaia, I. P. Grigor'eva, T. V. Chernik, and V. V. Gerbova (1986). Directors told me that they abided by the recommendations in these publications.

Representational art is strongly favored over free-form expression. Perhaps partially for this reason, children are not considered ready to express independent artistic creativity until they have acquired two prerequisites. The first is acquaintance with the objects they will be representing and appreciation for their aesthetic qualities. When appropriate, objects to be represented are brought into the classroom for viewing. Sometimes field trips are taken, for example, to see train tracks before drawing them. Poster and book illustrations are also heavily used. Upbringers are encouraged to speak enthusiastically while pointing out the aesthetic contributions of various design features, to teach the words for whole objects and their constituent parts, to sing songs and recite poems using these words, and to have children trace them in the air.

The second prerequisite for independent creativity is mastery of basic skills. These skills must be taught systematically, in small sequential steps. Because they have mastered so few skills, 2- and 3-year-old children are considered too young to be given much opportunity to follow their own inclinations. Opportunities for children to make their own decisions about what they will represent and how they will do it slowly increase, becoming more frequent beginning with the fifth year. At this time it is expected that children's self-directed work will incorporate the basic skills they have been taught.

Recall from Chapter 8 the methods used to motivate children. Upbringers often pretend that dolls and stuffed animals have brought the required materials and are watching the children work. Upbringers couch their instructions in play form so that children will think they are representing something rather than just practicing a fundamental skill. For example, when an upbringer begins a lesson for 2- or 3-year-olds on drawing curved lines, she might tell them to paint grass blowing in the wind.

What are the basic art skills children are expected to master? On the following pages, these skills, and some of the teaching methods used to achieve them, are described.

Drawing

One goal of drawing lessons is to teach correct usage of painting and drawing materials. Children are told to sit nicely with their backs straight. Right-handed children are taught to hold their paint brushes gently with the thumb, middle finger, and forefinger of the right hand. The palm of the left hand is supposed to rest on the top left corner of the paper to prevent it from slipping. (Left-handed children reverse this pattern.) Children learn to remove excess paint from their brushes by pressing them gently on the rim of a jar. They are told to use the whole sheet of paper, not just a small area of it. When they have finished painting, they rinse their brushes in water and blot them on paper. (Jars of water and blotting paper are provided on each table.) To cut down on mess, very young children are usually given gouache instead of regular paint. (Gouache is thick, like finger paint.)

Drawing lessons for 2-year-olds focus on teaching them how to make simple controlled marks on paper. Children are first taught how to press a paint brush onto paper to make neat dabs. After they have mastered dabbing, they practice making vertical lines, then horizontal lines, and finally curved lines. At the beginning of the year they are given one color of gouache at a time; later they are offered two colors. The importance of not mixing colors is stressed.

Lessons for 3-year-olds continue in the same vein. The following skills are sequentially taught: (1) drawing and connecting horizontal and vertical short and long lines (e.g., to represent a fence); (2) drawing curved forms and circles (e.g., to represent clouds or wheels); (3) connecting lines to circles (e.g., to represent the sun and its rays or a balloon on a string); (4) drawing squares and rectangles (e.g., to represent handkerchiefs); and finally (5) connecting squares or rectangles to circles (e.g., to represent a wagon with wheels). During lessons on drawing short lines, 3-year-olds are encouraged to set up a rhythmic pace, drawing many lines at once.

Toward the end of the year, instruction in drawing trees is initiated. Since this is understood to be very difficult for 3-year-olds, special training takes place. Children might be helped to imagine branches while lifting their arms over their heads to pretend to be trees; they might trace tree shadows in the snow or with chalk; together with the upbringer they might trace a tree in the air with their fingers.

Four-year-olds add ovals to their repertoire of shapes. At first they examine objects and drawings that are oval shaped, comparing them to the shapes they have previously mastered. They draw ovals in the air or with a dry brush. Later they draw oval-shaped objects, such as prunes. Practice drawing people begins as well.

Four-year-olds also learn how different colors and color combinations affect the expressiveness of pictures. Upbringers explain that bright colors, symmetrical patterns, and repetition of color and form contribute to the beauty of Russian folk carvings and weavings and show children how they can reproduce this on paper. Initially children are required to copy upbringers' designs, but later in the year they may create their own, using the shapes and principles they have been taught.

In their pictures, 4-year-olds are encouraged to draw more than one item on each page. For example, they might draw fish in an aquarium (rather than just fish), or birds eating seeds (rather than just birds). To encourage planfulness, a few children might be asked to tell the class what they will draw, what colors they will use, or the like.

Sculpture

Sculpture lessons acquaint 2-year-olds with the properties of clay (or plasticine). For example, they are shown that it can be rolled and squeezed, that one can tear off pieces and then rejoin them, that one can make things with these pieces (pretend candy, pencils for dolls, etc.). The upbringer demonstrates, and children try to copy what she has done. They roll clay between their palms to make cylinders and balls, join the ends of cylinders to make circles, flatten balls to make disks, and finally join two different clay shapes, for example, a cylinder with a disk to represent a mushroom.

Three-year-olds review the skills initiated the year before and learn how to make cones (e.g., to represent carrots), how to connect different shapes (e.g., a rabbit made of balls and a carrot made from a cone), and how to decorate items with little balls or cylinders or by pinching their edges to make scallops. Upbringers are urged to demonstrate one or two ways to sculpt the required shapes and to allow children some latitude in choosing their own methods of working.

Four-year-olds are taught how to make oval shapes from balls, how to use their fingertips to smooth out sculptures (3-year-olds used only their palms), how to decorate items with drips of clay, and how to sculpt animals in action (e.g., birds drinking water).

Appliqué

Twice-monthly lessons in appliqué begin when children are three years old. In the beginning of the year, the focus of lessons is on the proper technique for gluing. Since children of this age are not yet allowed to use scissors, upbringers supply pre-cut paper shapes. Children are taught to lay each piece colored side down, to apply glue from the center out to the edges, to use two hands when placing a piece in its designated spot, to carefully press it down carefully, and finally to wipe off excess glue with a rag. At first children are given only rounded forms to glue; later they progress to the more difficult task of gluing items that have corners and points.

Sometimes 3-year-olds glue together shapes to represent people, animals, or objects. First they assemble figures composed of pieces that differ in size but not geometric shape (e.g., snowmen). Later they make figures composed of different geometric shapes (e.g., wagons with wheels). When making something combining two or more shapes, children must arrange them in the order prescribed by the upbringer.

As part of the lessons, upbringers are to begin to teach 3-year-olds good taste, using as a starting point the determination of which color combinations are pleasing and which are not. Children are taught how to tastefully alternate shapes of different colors and sizes on strips of paper and how to make symmetrical designs on squares. They glue circles of the same color in a line before they practice alternating two colors.

Toward the end of the year, children are allowed more freedom to choose colors and to make what they wish. For example, they might be given envelopes with a variety of paper shapes and allowed to decide how to arrange them.

Four-year-olds cut out their own shapes. Since they have not done this in prior years, the first lessons of the school year focus on correct use of scissors. Once this has been mastered, children practice drawing and cutting out their own geometric shapes (circles, rectangles, squares, ovals, and triangles). They are taught to make circles by cutting off the corners of squares and rounding the edges. Similarly, ovals are made from rectangles. Cut-out shapes are glued together to make various figures (e.g., a rocket from a cylinder and a triangle). Like lessons for 3-year-olds, lessons for 4-year-olds stress the aesthetic value of symmetrical, repeated design arrangements.

One director was proud of an innovation at her center combining drawing, painting, and appliqué. She called it "collective art." To make a collective art work, each child drew a picture or colored in a pre-cut shape according to a common theme. The upbringer might do so, too. After all of the individual pieces were ready, the upbringer would paste them together in an attractive arrangement on a large piece of poster board to make a unified whole. Complaining that her center was not receiving the recognition it deserved for these creations, this director ventured a hope that I might spread the idea in the United States.

Construction

Two-year-olds participate in once-weekly lessons in construction. They watch and listen as the upbringer shows them how to lay blocks end-to-end or on top of each other to make roads, towers, fences, and simple doll furniture such as chairs, beds, and tables. After watching, they try to copy her models or build with her. The upbringer teaches the names of the various shapes of blocks (cubes, prisms, etc.) and the difference between the words *narrow* and *wide*.

Three- and 4-year-olds have construction lessons once every other week; these lessons alternate with lessons in appliqué. Three-year-olds learn how to make borders around rectangles and circles with evenly spaced or adjoining blocks (e.g., to represent a fence around a pond). They include more pieces and colors in their structures than 2-year-olds and begin to make modifications in upbringers' models (e.g., copy them, but on a larger scale). Toward the end of the year they may have opportunities to design and modify their own structures with little or no help from the upbringer. To encourage planfulness, upbringers are to help children think through the number and kinds of blocks they will need. However, they are to give fewer, shorter, and more general instructions than they would give to 2-year-olds.

Construction lessons for 4-year-olds include instructions on the relations between block arrangement and stability and how to modify structures to make them larger or smaller. Upbringers present fewer models than to younger children; 4-year-olds try to build according to a description alone (e.g., "Build a two-story house for these two dolls."). They make paper details to decorate block structures (e.g., windows for houses). During the second half of the year, lessons are given in making simple objects out of paper (flags, cards) and natural materials (twigs, nuts, etc.). There seems to be more leeway for children's creativity during construction lessons than during lessons in painting, sculpture, or appliqué.

Responsibilities of "Helpers"

In classrooms with children aged 4 1/2 and older, each day one or two children are assigned to be "helpers." After each lesson, helpers put away the paints, glue, clay, and other materials that were used during the lesson. Usually they stay inside a few minutes longer than the other children so that they can finish their chores. Typically it is seen as an honor to be a helper.

Sample Art Lessons

Two examples of art lessons follow. The first involved 2-year-olds in a lesson on drawing and combining circles and lines to make suns. The second involved 4-year-olds in an appliqué lesson glueing together circles and triangles to make chicks with beaks and legs. For an example of a lesson that encouraged more creativity, the reader is referred to the description in Chapter 8 of the lesson for 5-year-olds in sculpting vases.

There were 14 2 1/2- and 3-year-old children in the classroom this day. For lessons, they were divided into two smaller groups. While the first seven had their lesson, the others engaged in free play. This day the upbringer began the lesson by asking children to come to the window to see what a beautiful, sunny day it was. She then led them to a table. After the children had sat down, the upbringer recited a short poem about the sun and

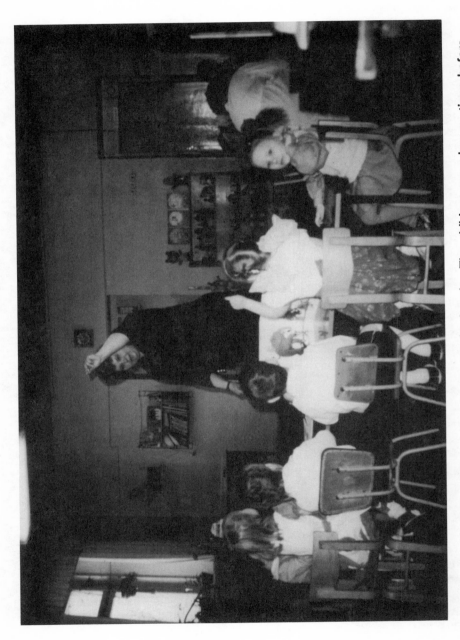

Photograph 13. An upbringer draws the sun in the air. The children copy her motions before attempting to draw the sun on paper.

pointed to some pictures of it on a bulletin board. She then opened a book and showed that the artist had drawn the sun on several of the pages.

Pointing to the sun on one of these pages, she asked the children, "What are these lines?" "Rays," some children called out. The upbringer nodded, "Right. Now we will draw the sun in the air. Watch me and copy what I do. Raise your right hand." She drew the sun in the air. "Draw around and around. Now look at the sun in the book. Now draw the rays with me from top to bottom." The children copied her motions in the air. (Photograph 13 was taken at this moment.)

Several of the children, however, kept turning to look at me, perhaps because they were interested in my camera. The upbringer cheerfully reminded them to pay attention to what she was doing. Picking up a yellow marker, she drew the sun on a piece of paper. It was a large circle with lines emanating from its periphery. "Look how I'm drawing," she said as she worked.

Next she gave each child a piece of paper and a yellow or orange marker (children could choose which of these two colors they wanted). "Draw the sun. Remember to hold the marker in your right hand. Hold it like this. Hold the paper down with your left hand," she reminded them. Then, remembering that one boy was left-handed, she corrected herself, "Dima is left-handed. He draws with his left hand."

Instructions were interspersed with compliments and exclamations to look at the good work other children were doing: "Good for you, Nadia!" "Look how Nadia is doing it." "What smart children! You understood correctly!" "And now make the rays. Make them wider. Make sticks. From top to bottom. There you go—smart boy! Draw sticks all around." "Now color it in so it will be pretty. Now draw the cute little rays." "Look how well Katia did it!"

One child's sun looked messy. The upbringer urged her to correct it: "Come on, draw nicely. There, good for you."

Children who were finished drawing left the table to find something to play with while the others worked. When all were finished, the upbringer called the group back together for the evaluation. She spread the children's drawings out on the table. With much inflection and enthusiasm in her voice, she praised the group, "You made good suns, and the most important thing is that you understood what you were supposed to do." One girl came in for a special compliment. The upbringer liked her sun so much that she drew a face on it. Then she dismissed the group. "Thank you. You drew so well. All the suns have made it so light in our room!"

A classroom of 4-year-olds sat four to a table, eyes on the upbringer. In front of each child was a green piece of paper about 8" X 10", a brush for glue, and a small square of paper on which to rest the brush. In the middle of each table was a small bowl with glue and a plate with shapes the upbringer had cut out earlier: eight yellow circles—four about 2" in diameter and four about half that size, and 12 small orange triangles, four about half the size of the others. There were also two pieces of pink paper on each table, each about 5" X 3". The upbringer was introducing a lesson in appliqué. She held a big toy duck.

UPBRINGER: "Who came?"
CHILDREN: "A duck!"
UPBRINGER: "How can you tell it's a duck?"
CHILD: "It's yellow."
CHILD: "It has wings."
CHILD: "It has a round body."
UPBRINGER [pointing to the duck's head]: "What's this?"
CHILDREN [in unison]: "Head."
UPBRINGER [pointing to the duck's beak]: "What's this?"
CHILDREN [in unison]: "Beak."
UPBRINGER [putting the duck down]: "Now I'll put the duck here so he can watch you. We are going to make ducks."

The upbringer now pointed to a brown paper she had tacked up on the wall. A yellow circle was glued to the middle of the paper. "Now look at this piece of paper. See, I glued a circle onto it. That will be the duck's torso. Now I will put a smaller circle on for the head. If I put it low, the duck will look sad. So I want to put it high."

Next the upbringer explained and demonstrated how to apply glue. "First you will take one of the larger circles from the plate. Place it upside down on the pink paper and dab some glue on it. Then turn the circle over and glue it onto the green paper. Then take a small circle and glue it slightly overlapping with the big circle. Press it down with two fingers. Now take one of the smallest orange triangles and glue it on the head on the side like this. It is the beak. Then use the bigger triangles for the feet."

A child asked, "What about a tail?"

The upbringer answered, "We won't put tails on today."

"Why?" the child persisted.

"There is no time. Well, if you have time, you can."

Now children got to work. The upbringer walked around the room, making comments: "Why are you doing it with one hand?" she asked one child. "It would be more comfortable with two." "Make sure your pieces are straight. Hold the circle with two hands," she counseled another.

"You have too much glue on your brush," a girl was reprimanded. "Wipe the excess on the edge of the bowl."

The children had some choice in sequencing: "You may glue the feet on first or the beak on first, however you'd like." Twice, when children asked how to put the beak or feet on, the upbringer answered, "However you'd like." Yet other comments indicated that she felt ambivalent about allowing children to make decisions. For example, I heard one boy admonished, "How will the duck walk if his legs are not in the right place? Take them off and reglue them before it's too late." Similarly, when she noticed that another child had applied glue only to the middle of the circles, not to the edges, she chided him, "You need to think with your head."

As children neared completion, the upbringer came around to draw in their ducks' eyes. Her voice slightly raised, she told those who were working slowly to hurry.

Children who were finished got up from their tables to arrange their papers on a long table for the evaluation. After most had finished, the upbringer came over. "You made very good ducks," she began. "But Sasha, where is your duck's beak?" When Sasha said he didn't know, she seemed vexed. "What do you mean you don't know?" she asked.

A boy who was fooling around during the lesson was told that he would have to stay inside until he had finished his duck. A boy and a girl were reminded that they were the classroom helpers today and should put away all of the brushes and bowls and throw away the pieces of paper used for catching excess glue. (See Photograph 18 in Chapter 12.) "When you help, help correctly," the upbringer told them. The other children went to the dressing room to prepare to go outside.

LANGUAGE, LITERATURE, AND THE SURROUNDING WORLD

One director told me that, in her opinion, small children today do not speak as well as children did 10 years ago. Enriching children's language experiences is therefore a priority. Ideally, this occurs throughout the day as upbringers make comments to children and engage them in conversation. Twice weekly there are also formal lessons specifically directed toward increasing children's vocabulary, improving their grammar, helping them articulate clearly and expressively, and teaching them to be polite, attentive listeners and conversational turn-takers (Gerbova, Zimonina, & Pushnina, 1986). Memorization of songs, stories, and poems is also encouraged.

Language development efforts are often embedded in literature and "getting to know the world around us" activities. The teaching style is usually didactic, and upbringers are taught to take advantage of the fact that young children are ready imitators. For example, the upbringer might read a story or poem, emphasizing certain words or sounds, and then ask the children to repeat the words, or even the whole story or poem. Sometimes the children act out the story line.

When the focus is on articulation, poems or actions that exercise particular sounds are presented. For example, if the sound "s" is to be practiced, children are told to pretend to be snakes. When the focus is on forming the plural, the upbringer might present pictures of single animals, then show pictures of several animals and ask children to provide the labels. When the focus is on helping children express their thoughts in well-connected sentences, "why," "when," and "how" questions are asked, or children are asked to describe what is happening in particular pictures. As children perfect speech sounds and grammatical forms, it is hoped that they are also developing a love for the Russian language and its literature.

A favorite activity is to have children pull items out of a "magic bag." As they take them out, they use nouns and adjectives to label and describe them (e.g., a small, yellow cup). The upbringer might call attention to the ways in which all of the objects are similar (e.g., all are used for eating) and the ways in which they are different (e.g., in color, in specific functions). A second round of this game might require the children to put a hand in the bag and guess what they are touching before they pull it out. In one version, I saw 2 1/2-year-old children tell what they wanted to pull out before they put their hands in. Memory and language were thus involved. (Children had to remember which objects had been put in the bag and which ones other children had already taken out.)

Sample Language, Literature, and Science Lessons

To communicate the flavor of training in this content area, below I have described four lessons. In the first, a Russian folk tale provided the opportunity to learn some words and to practice recitation skills:

A class of 3-year-olds sat on chairs arranged in a semicircle facing the upbringer. With the nanny's help, a stuffed tiger knocked at the door and entered the classroom. "Oh, look who is here!" the upbringer exclaimed. She reeled off a list of adjectives describing the tiger. "Isn't he nice! So fuzzy! So soft! So little! So clumsy!"

Then she asked the children to tell her about the tiger. The children called out adjectives, repeating those the upbringer had just used: "Little." "Clumsy." "Fuzzy."

UPBRINGER: "And what kind of eyes does he have?"
CHILD: "Black."
CHILD: "Shiny."
CHILD: "Little."
UPBRINGER: "Let's put him on the shelf so he can watch you. Everybody sit straight and pretty. Now everybody is looking at me attentively."

Using a flannel board, the upbringer told a story about a series of animals who found some boots in the woods and decided to try them on. The story had been chosen as a vehicle for teaching words for animal feet (paw, hoof, foot, and so on). The story was told with much expression. The props were attractive factory-produced paper pictures; pieces of flannel had been glued on the back so that the pictures would stay up on a flannel board. After the upbringer had finished telling the story, she asked the children to call out the words for puppies' feet, then roosters' feet, then ducks' feet, and the like. Then she proceeded to test both vocabulary and memory.

"Children, did you like the story? Yes? Do you want to hear it again?" she asked. The children agreed that they did. The upbringer started to retell the story, but this time every so often she stopped to ask the children what happened next. The children called out answers. One child was playing with a piece of paper. Wordlessly, the upbringer took it away.

The last part of the lesson involved solo recitations. "Who is brave and will retell the story all the way through?" the upbringer asked. When no one volunteered, she prodded, "Who is brave? Are you being shy? Don't be scared. I will help if you forget a part." One boy came to the front of the group and nearly flawlessly retold the story. He was profusely praised. After he sat down, a girl raised her hand. Though she tried hard, she missed a section and needed the upbringer's help. The upbringer praised her too: "Very good. You missed one section. But that's all right. Good for you." By the time the lesson had ended, four children had attempted to recite the story. One child, however, kept turning his head away, toward the window. The upbringer asked him, "Vania, what's the matter? This isn't interesting for you?" Vania started to pay attention, so by the end of the lesson the upbringer was able to say to the group, "Everybody did very well. Vania also did well. Tomorrow he'll do even better."

Another lesson focused on color words, on properties of water, and on why some objects sink while others float. This was an example of language training embedded in a science lesson:

Six 3-year-olds sat at a table for the afternoon lesson. On the table were two large bowls of water. The children waited patiently while the upbringer went over to a shelf to gather some hollow inch cubes.

Returning to the table, the upbringer started the lesson: "Everyone sit straight and pretty and listen carefully. What do I have?" Instead of answering, the children reached for the cubes. Gently stopping them, the upbringer told one child to take a white one. He did so. "Tell me what color it is," the upbringer required. "White," he answered. "Right. Now use it to scoop up some water from one bowl and spill it into the other." The child complied. "Did you get a lot or a little?" the upbringer asked him. "A little," he replied. The upbringer repeated this procedure until all six children had picked a cube and transferred water from bowl to bowl.

The upbringer now put the cubes away and brought out six small rocks. She gave each child one. "Are your rocks hard or soft?" she asked them. "Hard," they answered. Next they were instructed to individually drop their rocks in the water to see if they would sink or float. Then they did the same with feathers.

Turning to a different theme, the upbringer asked, "Why can you see the rocks even though they are covered with water?" When no one answered, she supplied the correct word, "Because water is *transparent*."

"Now let's put these plastic frogs in the water. Why do they float? Because they are *light*. Take a frog." As each child picked a frog, s/he was asked to identify its color. Some children tried to answer for those who were slow to respond. The upbringer stopped them, "He knows. Let him tell us what color frog he has."

The lesson continued:

UPBRINGER: "Now put your hands in the water. What can you say about the water?"
CHILD: "It's transparent."
UPBRINGER: "Right. What are your hands like now?"
CHILD: "Wet."
UPBRINGER: "Right."
CHILD: "Clean."
UPBRINGER: "Right."
Others copied the last two, calling out "wet" and "clean."
UPBRINGER [putting soap in the water]: "Now the water isn't transparent anymore. It is *murky*. So today we learned about water. Let's describe water."

CHILD: "Transparent."
UPBRINGER: "Yes, and what else?"
CHILD: "Dirty."
CHILD: "Murky."
UPBRINGER: "Right."
CHILD: "Clean."
CHILD: "Warm."
UPBRINGER: "And what else can water be like?"
CHILD: "Light."
CHILD: "Cold."
UPBRINGER: "Yes. Well good for all of you. You learned well."

In the following lesson, both poetry and science were used as the context for language training:

Ten 2-year-olds sat on chairs in a row facing their upbringer. They listened attentively as the upbringer recited a poem about birds. In answer to her question, "What was the poem about?" they called out, "birds." Next she showed them a series of poster-sized pictures of birds. For each one, she told the name of the bird (swallow, duck, parrot, etc.) and explained what it was doing (flying, pecking at seeds, drinking water, preening, feeding its babies, etc.). After the last picture, she asked some questions:

UPBRINGER: "What do all of the birds do?"
CHILD: "Fly."
CHILD: "Drink."
CHILD: "Peck."
UPBRINGER: "Good for you! What kinds of birds did I show you?"
CHILD: "Swallow."
CHILD: "Rooster."

Now the upbringer told them she had a surprise for them and left the room for a few seconds. The children remained seated, quietly waiting. The upbringer came back holding a bird cage with a parakeet inside. "Come up to the cage but I must tell you to be quiet," she told the children. The children surrounded the cage, very interested.

The upbringer continued, "See how she is scared. Don't touch the cage. We don't want to scare her. What color are the feathers on her breast?"

A child answered, "Blue."

"Yes, blue. Look how she can play. Look how she's not scared now because you are all being so quiet."

The parakeet fluttered around the cage a little.   "What's she doing now?" the upbringer asked, lowering her voice almost to a whisper.

"Flying," some children answered.

"What does she eat?"

"Seeds."

Next the children were asked to sit back down on their chairs.

UPBRINGER: "What can birds do?"

CHILD: "Fly."

CHILD: "Peck."

CHILD: "Clean themselves."

Some children scooted their chairs closer to the cage so that they could see better. The upbringer was understanding: "I know you want to sit closer." She helped them rearrange their chairs so that they could see as she filled the bird's seed container.

Finally the children were given headbands with pictures of birds on the front.   They got up and ran around the room with arms outspread, pretending to be birds. Every so often (at the upbringer's suggestion) they stopped to bend down and peck. After about two minutes of this, the upbringer ended the lesson by bringing out a stuffed toy cat. As if on cue, the children ran away from her, screaming and laughing.

Language lessons for 5-year-olds are more demanding, requiring concept development as well as memory.   One that I observed focused on names for animals.

The children sat school-like, at desks arranged in pairs.   The teacher stood in front of them. "Sit prettily. Everyone is looking at me attentively," the upbringer began.   She introduced a guessing game; children were to guess the name of the animal she was describing (e.g., "I give children milk. When I am hungry, I moo. When I am full, I am quiet.").   Unlike younger children, these children were to raise their hands and wait their turn to speak. They raised their hands in the traditional Russian fashion: right upper arm parallel to the desk and forearm at a right angle with the upper arm; some placed the left hand under the elbow of the right arm.

After the guessing game came one in which the children were shown pictures of four animals at a time (e.g., horse, cow, goat, and bear) and asked which one did not belong with the others. The correct answer was always the wild animal (in this case the bear). A discussion of the meaning of the word "domesticated" followed.

UPBRINGER: "Why are domestic animals called domestic?" [Calls on Misha.]

MISHA: "Because they live at home."

UPBRINGER: "Think some more."

UPBRINGER [after no one volunteered another answer]: "How do we care for domestic animals?"

CHILDREN [not waiting to be called on, in chorus]: "Feed them."

UPBRINGER: "I didn't call on anyone yet." [Calls on Lena.]

LENA: "Give them water."

UPBRINGER: "Yes." [Calls on Dima.]

DIMA: "Let them come inside."

UPBRINGER: "Right. How do we care for wild animals?" [Silence.] We take care of domesticated animals. Some are house pets and some are needed for food. Wild animals take care of themselves and do not live with us."

Next the upbringer gave each child a picture of a baby animal. As she held up pictures of individual adult animals, the children with pictures of the young of that species were to hold them up and tell their names (e.g., "puppies" for dogs, "kids" for goats). When children could not remember the correct words, the upbringer smiled and supplied them. After this part of the lesson was over, the upbringer praised the group, "Good for you. All of you tried." To end the lesson, the upbringer gave each child a piece of white paper and some colored pencils. They were to draw their favorite animals.

MATHEMATICAL CONCEPTS

Lessons in "elementary mathematical concepts" begin when children are 2 1/2 to 3 years old. Activities focus on counting and simple arithmetic, size comparisons, identification of geometric forms, distance relations, and time concepts. Many of the lessons include exercises in classification. It is thought that without such exercises, young children will continue to perceive globally; they will not tease out the individual elements of stimuli. The upbringer is therefore to call attention to the various attributes of objects. She is to explain that, depending on the particular task, some characteristics of objects are relevant, while others are not. For example, the number of sides is relevant but color is irrelevant to the determination of shape. Two- to 3-year-olds are expected to be able to keep only one attribute in mind at a time (e.g., shape *or* color); 4- to 5-year-olds are to work on keeping two attributes in mind simultaneously (e.g., shape *and* color).

I shall describe now the goals of lessons in this area and a sample of corresponding activities. These activities are recommended by Zinaida Boguslavskaia and Elena Smirnova (1991), V. V. Danilova and N. A. Piskareva (1986), and Leonid Venger, Ol'ga D'iachenko, Roxana Govorova, and Liubov Tsekhanskaia (1989). In the interests of brevity, I have combined some subareas. Goals and recommended lessons in counting, simple arithmetic, and size comparisons are discussed together under the heading "number concepts." Identification of geometric forms and distance relations are discussed together under the heading "spatial relations." The section concludes with descriptions of two lessons that I observed.

Number Concepts

Number lessons for 2 1/2- to 3-year-olds are focused on simple size and quantity comparisons. The goals are to teach children to distinguish between "more," "less," and "equal," and between "one," "many," and "none." Children are to learn to compare objects of different heights or widths or lengths. Only one of these dimensions is to be taken into account at a time. Learning the vocabulary denoting relative size (e.g., the word *more*) is an important part of the lessons.

Examples of specific lesson activities for 2 1/2- to 3-year-olds include (a) placing several blocks on a table and asking children to pick out the *one* block just like the one the upbringer is holding; (b) having children divide a group of items into two piles: those that are *big* and those that are *little*; and (c) having children notice that there are *many* of certain items in the room (e.g., chairs) but only *one* of other items (e.g., aquarium).

The goals of number lessons for 4-year-olds involve teaching them to count accurately from left to right up to five items, to use ordinal counting for series of items (i.e., "first," "second," etc.), and to place in order three items differing in size. Children of this age are to learn to separate size from other characteristics of objects (e.g., noticing that two flags might be the same size even though they are different in color). Upbringers are also to teach elementary principles of conservation of number (e.g., that two rows have the same number of items even though one row occupies more space because the items in it are further apart).

Activities during number lessons for 4-year-olds might include (a) presenting children with variously colored ribbons of two different sizes and asking them to figure out which ones could be used as belts for a teddy bear and which ones could be used as belts for a doll; (b) having children order a set of nested dolls (*matreshki*) according to size; and (c) showing children four toy squirrels and five toy trees, counting them, discussing the fact that there are more trees than squirrels, then adding one squirrel and pointing out that now the number of squirrels equals the number of trees, and finally spreading the squirrels apart and counting them to show that the number of squirrels remains the same no matter how they are positioned. In each case the upbringer is to direct the lesson by showing the children what to do and by asking a series of closed questions (i.e., questions having only one right answer).

Spatial Concepts

Lessons on spatial concepts for 2 1/2- to 3-year-old children focus on teaching them to distinguish and label two geometric forms (circles and squares), and to understand and use words denoting relative position ("in front of," "behind," "below," "above," "left," and "right").

Lessons might involve children in (a) running their fingers around pictured squares and circles, (b) identifying squares and circles in a "magic bag" by feel alone; (c) dressing dolls while describing the relative position of the various body parts and the correct orientation of each piece of clothing; and (d) playing games requiring participants to wave their right hands, then their left hands, then touch the child in front of them, and so on.

Triangles as well as circles and squares are to be included in 4-year-olds' lessons on geometric shapes. In addition, practice continues with words denoting orientation in space. Examples of spatial lessons for this age group include (a) incorporating location words (e.g., "below," "to the right of," etc.) in the hints given children as they search for toys that have been hidden in the classroom; (b) repositioning a set of objects while children have their eyes closed, then asking them to figure out and explain what was changed; and (c) having children pick out a shape (e.g., triangle) from an array of variously colored and sized triangles, circles, and squares (so that they will understand that shape is not dependent on color or size).

Temporal Concepts

Finally, upbringers are to concern themselves with children's understanding of simple temporal concepts. Two-and-a-half and 3-year-olds are to learn the correct use of the words *morning, day, evening,* and *night.* Four- and 5-year-olds are to learn the order of parts of the day (morning after night, etc.). They are also to learn to understand and use the words *yesterday, today,* and *tomorrow.*

Throughout the day upbringers are encouraged to use temporal words with both age groups as they talk to children about past, present, and future events. Pictures, stories, and poems can be used during lessons to elicit temporal language. For example, while showing children a poster, the upbringer can ask them questions such as, "What is this child doing?" "What time of day do you think it is?" "When do you do this?"

Sample Lessons in Mathematical Concepts

The reader might note the role of the dolls in both of the following lessons:

Five 2-year-olds (a third of the class) sat at a table with their upbringer. The nanny brought over a doll, Katia, five wooden shape inlay boards, five solid wooden cubes and five solid wooden spheres. She explained that Katia would like to watch the children learn about shapes. The upbringer welcomed Katia, telling her that, yes, she could stay, and sat her next to her on one end of the table. Then she gave each child a board. Each board had circle- and square-shaped holes. (See Photograph 14.)

"What do you see on the boards?" the upbringer asked. Not waiting for an answer, she went on, "Different kinds of holes. Point to a circle." She kept repeating the instruction, addressing individual children as needed, until every child had pointed to a circle. "Now point to a square." Again she repeated herself until every child had pointed correctly. Then she placed some wooden spheres and cubes in the middle of the table and told the children that they were to put a sphere in the circular hole and a cube in the square hole. "Good for you!" she praised those who got it right. In most cases she did not criticize when children made mistakes. Just once, when one boy put his sphere in a square hole, she complained, "Maxim, you aren't thinking."

Katia (the doll) helped keep order. At one point a boy took for himself all of the spheres and squares. "Katia wants you to put them back in the middle," the upbringer remarked in a singsong, motherly voice. "Just take

Photograph 14. Two-year-olds participate in a lesson on geometric shapes. Note the doll next to the upbringer.

one. Leave some for the others." One boy started dropping his ball on the table. The upbringer explained why he shouldn't do this: "Alesha, don't knock. You are distracting the other children."

One child sat watching, looking baffled. "Sashka [very affectionate diminutive of *Alexander*], look what the others have done. Now you do it. Take one ball. Where does it go? You can do it. Everyone else has done it."

The upbringer talked almost constantly, coaxing and repeating herself until each child had performed correctly. Finally all of the spheres and cubes were in their right places.

"Now everyone pick up a ball. Try to roll it," the upbringer instructed. The children tried it. "Now pick up a cube. See if the cube will roll. Does it roll? No. But the ball does. It is round." The children never said a word. The upbringer answered her own questions.

"What are these called?" she continued, holding up a sphere. "Little balls," she explained. "What are these called? Cubes."

"You are so good. So smart." The lesson was over. The children were reminded to push their chairs in under the table as they left. The upbringer's voice was kindly as she called back one girl who had forgotten.

Fifteen 4-year-olds participated together in a lesson on shape and number concepts. The director of this center observed with me. "It makes it hard, having so many children at once," she whispered.

A toy telephone "rang." The upbringer answered. "It's Burratino!" she told the children. "He wants to come in!" The nanny appeared with Burratino (a doll resembling Pinocchio) and a box of flat wooden pieces shaped like pie sections. The upbringer instructed the children to group the shapes by color "to show Burratino." As the children worked, the upbringer commented, "We're doing it to show Burratino." After the shapes had been grouped by color, the next step was to make a circle out of them. The upbringer helped those who were having difficulty. Noticing that the children seemed crowded at the table, she suggested that some work on the rug.

One child complained that another had bumped her.

"Was it an accident?" the upbringer asked. The children did not answer, and there was no further discussion.

"How many pieces do we need to make a circle?" the upbringer continued with the lesson. "Two!" guessed some. "Four!" said others. "Five!" Finally, a boy called out the correct number, six. "Golden one! Smart boy! Good for you! Right!" the upbringer enthused.

"What does yellow remind you of?"

"The sun," answered a child.

"Now everyone look at me. What is this?"

"Circle!"

"Now if I break it into two halves what do I get?"

"Two pieces," someone called out.

"Right. Now let's play bubble." All but one of the children stood up and made a circle. One girl stayed at the table to work on the shapes. She was permitted to do so.

"Good," said the upbringer. Now look at my right hand. The one you eat with. Who is on your right?" The children were to name the child on their right. Some were correct; some not. Those who were wrong were gently corrected.

Next the upbringer put some wooden flowers on the floor. The children counted with her as she lay them out. "You are the butterflies. Are there more flowers or more butterflies?" she asked. There was no answer. "Let's fly, please." The children ran on their tiptoes around the flowers. When the upbringer told them to stop, each stepped on a flower. "Are there enough flowers now for the butterflies?" "Yes," the children replied in chorus. "Yes, so the number of butterflies and the number of flowers are equal," the upbringer explained.

"Does anyone need to go to the bathroom?" asked the upbringer. "Where are the men who will help me move the tables?" While some children left for the bathroom, a few boys helped the upbringer move the tables back to their original places (they had been put side-by-side for the lesson). Then both sexes helped her arrange the chairs in a semicircle. Those who helped were praised profusely. Then children were asked to sit down on the chairs. "Let's see what Burratino brought us," the upbringer said as she peeked in a basket. "Oh! *Baranki*!" (*Baranki* are similar to bread sticks, but round).

"Do you want a whole or a half *baranka*?" she asked the group.

"A whole," the children answered.

"Can I make one into two halves?" She broke one into two to show that it could be done.

"Now how can I make it into a whole?" Holding the two halves together, she demonstrated how they fit together to make a whole.

"If I break each half again, how many pieces will I have?" Breaking each half, she counted with the children: "one, two, three four."

The lesson was almost over. Each child was given a piece of *baranka* to eat. Each said thank you as s/he received his or her piece. Showing the empty basket, the upbringer asked, "How many pieces are there now?" "Zero!" she answered her own question.

Now she gave each child a piece of candy. "Can I divide a piece of candy?" she asked as she handed them out.

"Yes," a child answered.

"Yes," agreed the upbringer, "but it will be difficult to do. Why?"

"Because they are hard," someone called out.

"Smart children!" "And where will we put the trash?" The children ran to the bathroom to throw away their candy wrappers. Now it was time to go outside.

MUSIC

This is the one content area taught by specialists, not by classroom upbringers. "Music upbringers" worked in all of the centers in which I observed. The largest center had two full-time music upbringers; in others they worked part-time. In all but the smallest center, music lessons took place in a large room otherwise reserved for holiday celebrations, parent meetings, and so forth. The only furniture in this room was a piano and child-sized chairs. In the smallest center there was no such room, and the music lessons were held in the playroom. (In this center both playrooms had pianos.)

Music lessons lasting about 20 to 25 minutes begin when children are 1 1/2 to 2 years old. For all preschool age-groups, the primary goal is to foster a love and appreciation for music. Secondary goals are to develop in children the ability to hear moods, rhythms, and representations in vocal and instrumental music; to sing clearly and with expression; to move in rhythm with music; and to learn some beginning dance steps. Beginning when children are 4, they learn how to play simple musical instruments such as triangles, cymbals, spoons, and xylophones. Several times a year children show off these skills in gala holiday performances for parents.

The early childhood literature (Grigor'eva, 1986a, 1986b; Radynova, 1990) reminds music upbringers that the atmosphere during music lessons should be cheerful and energetic; children should be enjoying themselves. I found this to be very much the case except in one center in which the music upbringer was very short with the older children. She later told me that she was on edge because of personal worries connected with the country's current economic crisis. She was also worried that the children would not perform well for parents at the upcoming May Day celebration.

As in the other content areas, the goals of music lessons differ by age-group. As indicated by Grigor'eva (1986a, 1986b) music lessons for 2-year-olds are to acquaint them with short instrumental pieces and songs on familiar themes. Songs are repeated many times so that children will get to know them well. Music upbringers point out how music can represent real-life sounds such as a horse galloping, rain falling, an airplane roaring. To become aware of rhythm, she leads children in clapping their hands, tapping their feet, or waving flags or handkerchiefs to music. Sometimes children act out the theme and tempo of songs; for example, they might pretend to glide through the air like birds or drive a car in time with the music. So that they become aware of the beginning and end points of musical pieces, child might march to music, starting and stopping when it starts and stops.

Two-year-olds play simple games such as hide-and-go-seek and "rabbits and foxes" (a chase game) to appropriate music. Didactic games are sometimes used. Children listen to music and guess the name of the song, whom it's about (a bear or a cat, for example), tell whether it is loud or quiet, fast or slow, sounds like a bear or a horse, and so forth. They listen to several instruments individually (rattles, tambourines, bells, and drums are favorites for this age-group), then identify them when the music upbringer plays them from behind a curtain.

Simple dance steps are also taught. In one center I observed as 2-year-olds were taught to pair off and, facing each other and holding hands, to tap their heels in rhythm to music. Later they danced with dolls. Afterward, the dolls stayed to watch the rest of the lesson. The literature reminds music upbringers that children of this age are slow to follow directions and that great patience and warmth are required if lessons are to go well. Classroom upbringers should sing and dance with the children rather than just watch.

Music lesson goals and teaching methods for 3-year-olds are much the same as those for 2-year-olds. They include continued practice in starting and stopping on signal, listening to music that expresses feelings and represents familiar sights and sounds, moving in rhythm with music, and recognizing drums, tambourines, and rattles by sound. In addition, upbringers are to help 3-year-olds enunciate clearly and draw out sounds while singing.

More is demanded of 4-year-olds than of the younger age-groups. To develop listening skills, music upbringers have children compare two musical pieces according to their themes, rhythms, and moods. They are to learn to carry tunes correctly and to articulate words clearly; they are to know how to sing one or one-and-a-half tones higher or lower than the original melody. Four-year-olds are taught to sing "in subgroups"; half the children are silent while the other half sings one verse or couplet, then the first group is silent while the other group sings.

Four-year-olds learn to shake rattles and tambourines and clap wooden spoons in rhythm to music. They also learn to play tunes on the xylophone. Sometimes the class plays in "subgroups," much as in singing. They practice traditional folk dance steps. There are some opportunities for improvisation, but most of the lesson is spent in learning songs and dances chosen by the music upbringer. Photograph 15 shows children demonstrating a dance they have learned. The photograph was taken during a May Day celebration at one of the centers.

Sample Music Lessons

Below I describe three of the music lessons that I observed. The first was for 2-year-olds, the second for 3-year-olds, and the third for 4-year-olds.

I was seated in the music room, waiting with the music upbringer, when a classroom upbringer arrived with 10 children. Most were two years old, but a few were several months younger. "Say hello," the upbringer cheerfully reminded the children. "Hello," they complied in chorus, both to me and to the music upbringer. "Hello, cute little children," the music upbringer returned the greeting.

Now the classroom upbringer left the room for a few seconds. When she returned, she was holding a doll. The doll (with the upbringer's help, of course) said hello to each child individually, then indicated that she would like to play hide-and-go-seek. The upbringer agreed that this would be a good idea. Still holding the doll, she left the room again for a few seconds. This time she returned rolling a child-sized car with the doll in the driver's seat. Next to the doll were 10 small flags. (The flags used in music lessons do not have national emblems. The cloth may be a rectangle, a triangle, or composed of several streamers in blue, red, pink, yellow, and/or green.)

Each child was given a flag. As the music upbringer played a simple tune, the children waved them, singing, "lya, lya lya lya," in time with the music. Then, when the music stopped, they were to hide from the doll by holding the flags in front of their faces. When the music started again, they were to resume their flag waving. One child started to play with the car instead. The upbringer gently moved him away, saying, "Leave the car; come hide from the doll with us. We'll bring the car into our classroom later. You can play with it then." Another child did not participate at all.

She was allowed to wander and watch. "She's new and only 1 1/2 years old," the upbringer explained to me.

The hiding game lasted a few minutes. After it was over, the upbringer collected the flags and went out of the room for another few seconds. This time she returned with 10 nearly identical dolls. Each child was given a doll and instructed to dance with her, holding both of her hands as if she were a dancing partner. The upbringer demonstrated. Then, as the music upbringer played on the piano and sang, "*Chok, chok, kabluchok*," ("tap, tap, little heel"), the classroom upbringer and the children tapped their heels to the floor in rhythm with the music.

"Now the dolls will sit on the chairs and watch us dance," announced the music upbringer. The regular upbringer took the dolls from the children and seated them on the chairs lining one wall of the room. "Boys are supposed to invite girls to dance," she noted. Since the children were much too young for this to happen spontaneously, she paired them up herself. "Hold her hand firmly; you're a boy," she told one little fellow as she motioned for him to hold his partner's hand. There were more boys than girls, so one couple was made up of boys only, and one boy became the upbringer's partner. Facing their partners and holding both their hands, the upbringer and the children tapped their heels in time to the music. "*Chok, chok, kabluchok*," sang the upbringer as she demonstrated.

The lesson was now over, and the children were told to say good-bye to the dolls. Instead, however, several complained that they wanted to play with them some more. The upbringer asked the music upbringer if they could take the dolls to the classroom for a while. "We'll return them later." The music upbringer agreed and the children left happily, each holding a doll.

Accompanied by their upbringer, a group of 3-year-olds entered the music room. The music upbringer was waiting for them. After they had said hello to each other, she gave each child a little flag. Boys got darker ones than girls. "Sasha, you get a navy blue one. You're a man. You need a more somber one," she explained to one boy. Children were reminded to hold the flags in their right hands. Then the music upbringer sat down to play the piano. The children were to march to loud music, tiptoe to soft music. They were to stop when the music stopped. Their upbringer marched with them. "You were stepping well!" the music upbringer complimented them after they were finished. For the second part of the lesson, the children performed a three-step dance: in rhythm with the music they tapped their heels on the floor, clapped, twirled around, then repeated the sequence. Their hands were to be on their hips and their backs straight. "*Chok, chok, kablychok*," sang the music upbringer. After this dance with its clear expectations, the children were told to dance "any way you want" to a short piece the music upbringer played on the piano. Some walked, some swayed, some ran; clearly they felt comfortable in unstructured as well as in structured dancing.

Next the music upbringer played several songs on the piano, and the children were to remember their titles. One song was about a cat. After it was played, a boy was given a toy stuffed toy cat to hold. He held it the wrong way. "No, hold her this way; that way hurts her," the upbringer corrected him as she showed him how to hold the toy cat gently. The next song was about a bear, and another child was given a teddy bear to hold. When it was time for him to give the bear up, he didn't want to. His upbringer coaxed him, "Mishka is too heavy to hold for long. Put him on a chair." The child complied.

Now the upbringer told the children to come stand near the piano to sing with her. "Backs straight! Cute little arms down at your sides so they won't be in the way. There, good for you!" After she and the children had sung three songs together, she praised them: "Good for you! You sang in such a friendly manner!" She patted those standing closest to her. The last piece was wordless, but the music upbringer told the children that it was about a cat. They were to pretend they were cats, meowing to the music any way they wished.

One child did not want to participate. When the others stood up to sing, he remained seated. No one asked him to stand. The center director, who was seated next to me, whispered, "You're a psychologist. You see, one child does not want to participate."

Next they practiced a dance for the upcoming May Day celebration. A teddy bear (Mishka) had brought colorful little scarves for the children. Each child was given one. A large vase with birch branches was placed in the middle of the floor. Boys were to invite girls to be their partners. In twos, they practiced dancing to a song about rain and sunshine. Holding their scarves up in the air in their right hands, they walked in rhythm to the music around the vase, then at certain points stopped, faced their partners, hid their faces behind their handkerchiefs, then lowered the handkerchiefs, and, looking at their partners, stomped their feet and bowed to each other. After this dance was over, the boys were to escort the girls back to their seats.

The last event of the music lesson was a game. A long scarf was stretched out on the floor and chairs were placed on one side of it. The scarf represented a creek, and the chairs represented nests. The children pretended to be baby sparrows, and their regular upbringer pretended to be their mother. The music upbringer was a cat. Everyone stood on the other side of the creek from the nests. One child, the "main sparrow," flew back and forth over the creek while the others watched. Then suddenly the "cat" meowed and ran toward the "baby sparrows." The "mother bird" called for her "baby sparrows" to fly quickly over the creek. Screaming and laughing, they ran back to their "nests" to sit down. This game was repeated several times, to everyone's delight. When it was all over, the music upbringer asked the children, "Did you like this game?" "Yes," they answered.

"Oh, Mishka is saying something to me," the upbringer exclaimed, just as the group was about to leave. Holding the teddy bear, she whispered to him as if in conference. Turning to the children, she confided, "He says you were all so good. Sasha and Lena and Dima and . . . " she went on until she had named each of the children.

"The music lesson is finished. Good-bye," the music upbringer ended the lesson. "Good-bye," replied the children.

Fifteen 4-year-olds stood expectantly in front of the music upbringer. "First we will exercise," she told them. They rolled their heads from side to side, tiptoed in place, and pretended to wash their hands.

"Now our ears will get some exercise. And your feet may do whatever the music tells them to." The enthusiasm in the music upbringer's voice convinced me that she thoroughly enjoyed her work. As she played the piano, the children danced free form. When the music stopped, they sat down on child-sized chairs lined up against the wall. "Now march any way you want," the music upbringer told them. The children stood up again and marched in time to the music.

"Good for you," the music upbringer complimented them. But then she qualified her praise, "Whose cute little feet aren't obedient?" No one answered. "Almost everyone listened," the music upbringer agreed.

It was time for a didactic game. The music upbringer asked the children to sit down again. She held up a picture of the sun. "Is the sun happy or sad?" she asked. "Happy," answered the children. "Yes. The sun's cute little eyes are kind." Each child was given a card with a picture of the sun. Next the children were given cards with pictures of gray clouds. Holding up her picture of a cloud, the music upbringer asked, "Is the cloud happy or sad?" "Sad," answered the children. "Yes," agreed the music upbringer. She proceeded to explain the rules of the game: "I am going to play some music. If it sounds happy, hold up your card with the sun. If it sounds sad, hold up your card with the cloud. Now we will see how attentive you are."

Most of the children played correctly and were praised. Not all, however, managed to show the right card each time. Still sounding cheerful, the music upbringer remarked that "Some children are right. Some are wrong. Tanya's head is not working."

The last piece was a "happy" one. "Does this music make you feel happy or sad?" she asked. "Happy," the children responded. "Right. Now everyone is in a good mood. What does the music make you want to do?" "Dance," answered a child.

The children were now told to line their chairs up in rows near the piano. The music upbringer brought out some rattles and tambourines. Individual children asked for particular instruments; the music upbringer tried to accommodate their wishes. "Let's make it quiet," she said. The children held their instruments still. The instructions continued: "I will play the piano. First only the rattles will play with me. Then only the tambourines. Then everyone together. I will tell you when to play." The music upbringer sat down at the piano and signalled the rattles to play in rhythm with her. The children followed her instructions smoothly and were commended, "You all are helping me in such a friendly way."

"What is it called when many instruments are played together?" she asked.

"Orchestra," the children responded.

"What is the leader called?"

"Conductor."

"Now let's put the instruments away carefully so that we will have them for next time." The children returned the instruments.

"Now we are going to sing. Stand up prettily. Good. The girls are tender and smiling." The children gathered at one side of the piano. "I am going to sing a song. Listen carefully so you can tell me what it is about." Accompanying herself on the piano, the music upbringer sang. The children listened attentively; they appeared to be enjoying themselves. When the song was finished, a child correctly explained that it was about sparrows in the spring. The music upbringer followed by playing and singing the song slowly, stopping after every line so that the children could repeat after her. "Sing clearly, clearly," she reminded them. "All the girls are tender and smiling," she observed approvingly.

The last song was to be at the children's request. "What song would you like?" the music upbringer asked. One boy wanted to sing a song about Grandfather Frost. "Oh, that was so long ago," she objected. "It's March now. Let's sing something more recent." Another child's suggestion to sing a song about mothers was accepted. (It was just two weeks after International Women's Day.)

The last structured event of the music lesson was a dance. The children had practiced this dance many times and knew it well. A girl, Sveta, was chosen to start it. Everyone else was seated; Sveta was to select a partner. "Whom will she invite?" wondered the music upbringer. "Probably the most obedient boy." Sveta approached a boy and bowed to him. He got up and the two of them danced together, twirling and stomping. A minute or so later it was time for each of them to choose new partners. And so it went until all of the children were dancing. Most, but not all, of the couples were of mixed sex.

"Good for you. You listened well," the music upbringer complimented the group. "Since you are such cheerful, smiling children, I brought you a tape. Dance however you like." To my surprise, the tape was of rock 'n

Photograph 15. At a May Day celebration, children perform a dance. For weeks, during music lessons, they practiced the steps.

roll music. It was their reward for performing well during the lesson. (I was later to see this ending to music lessons in another center, also.) When the tape ended, the lesson was over.

PHYSICAL EDUCATION

Each week children participate in physical education lessons led by their regular upbringers. Typically there are two indoor and one outdoor lessons each week. The two indoor lessons take place in the playroom or, if the center has one, in the gym. Indoor lessons are held during the regular lesson times; outdoor lessons take place during the morning outside time.

Physical education classes have physical and psychological goals. The physical goals involve the development of the muscular and nervous systems. Much attention is paid to developing good posture and balance and to preventing flat-footedness. Special breathing exercises are used to increase lung capacity and encourage controlled, rhythmic breathing. Games train quick reaction times and the ability to start and stop on signal. Strength, stamina, flexibility, and differentiation and coordination of the large and small muscles are also stressed.

The psychological goals of physical education classes are social, emotional, and cognitive: willingness to act in concert with others, attentiveness to the needs of others for space and materials, willingness to follow directions, ability to follow simple game rules, accurate judgment about distance and direction, and a beginning sense of time.

It stands to reason that more is expected of children as they grow older. Older children spend more time in each activity, and movements are expected to be more complex. A sampling of expectations for 2-, 3-, and 4-year-olds follows. The information on goals and specific activities was drawn from a chapter by V. N. Andreeva and D. V. Khukhlaeva (1986), and from a book on the subject by Praskovia Bytsinskaya, Valentina Vasiukova, and Galina Leskova (1990).

Goals for 2-year-olds include learning how to participate with the group and without bothering others; developing proper posture (walking with the head held high and not shuffling); developing the ability to keep one's balance while running, walking, and stepping across a balance beam; developing the arches of the foot; increasing stamina (to 40 seconds of uninterrupted running); learning to jump high with two feet and land on the toes; learning to learning to jump high with two feet and land on the toes; learning to throw and roll a ball with one hand and two hands; learning to throw a ball into a basket a foot and a half away; practicing crawling on the stomach and on hands and knees; and climbing a few rungs on a climbing apparatus. Frequent repetition of movements (but with changing play form themes) is recommended.

Physical education classes for 3-year-olds include drills in forming single-file lines and circles. Often children exercise in these formations. Children practice walking on tiptoes with the knees held high, turning on command, sustained fast and slow running, jumping down from heights of 15 to 20 centimeters, jumping in a half-squatting position, distance jumping, throwing a ball horizontally one meter at a target, catching balls after bouncing them on the floor or throwing them in the air, climbing up the rungs of a climbing apparatus, crawling between objects and under boards, and keeping one's balance while running and walking on narrow paths or on balance beams. Outside, children are taught how to ride tricycles correctly.

Four-year-olds practice dividing up into two, three, or four parallel lines and following the leader of one's own line. Attention is giving to proper walking: arms and legs should move together, the head should be held high, the back straight. Children are to practice walking on their heels and on the sides of their feet; they alternate fast with slow walking and walking with running. The focus of running exercises is on developing stamina and good form (lifting the legs from the hips, energetically pushing off the floor with the toes). While jumping, 4-year-olds are expected to coordinate the movements of their arms and legs; they are also introduced to hopping on one foot and to jumping rope.

Four-year-olds are taught proper hand, arm, and leg positions for throwing, rolling, and catching balls. Practice in crawling on one's stomach using the hands and feet for locomotion continues. Children use this type of crawl to creep under rods and over balance beams. They climb ladders in order to conquer fear of low heights and learn how to climb up and down safely. Exercises such as walking on balance beams, walking across blocks while holding something, and standing on tiptoes or on one foot as long as possible are included to develop balance. Physical education lessons for this age-group often conclude with an active game with rules, such as tag.

Sample Physical Education Lessons

Descriptions of two physical education classes follow. Both took place indoors. The first involved 2-year-olds, the second, 3- and 4-year-olds.

A group of 2-year-olds walked into the gym with their upbringer. Their first task was to undress. The children sat down on chairs lined up on one side of the room and worked on taking off their shoes, socks, shirts, shorts, and dresses. Most needed some help from the upbringer. As they undressed, they left their shoes on the floor in front of their chairs and the rest of their clothes on the chairs. Clad only in undershirts and underpants, they were ready for their lesson.

The lesson began with some exercises in pretend form. "You are beetles," the upbringer instructed. "When I say 'beetles fly,' you must fly a little, then stoop down." She demonstrated, running with arms outstretched, then stopping to kneel.

After the children had been beetles for a few minutes, the upbringer announced that Katia, a doll, had arrived with rattles for everyone. Katia was placed on the floor, and the children were told to form a circle around her. Each child was given a rattle. On signal from the upbringer, they hid the rattles behind their backs, then stretched their torsos and arms forward to show Katia the rattles.

After a minute or so of this, the upbringer changed the activity. "Let's show Katia how we can be small," she said. Everyone squatted. "Now let's show her how we can be big." Everyone stood up. "Now bend down to pick a dandelion." Everyone squatted again. Standing and squatting was repeated several times. The next exercise was for the lungs. Pretending to hold a dandelion, the upbringer instructed, "Blow the dandelions. Blow hard." The children blew at their fingers.

"Now everyone sit on the floor. Stretch your legs out in front of you. Put your rattle on the floor in front of your legs. Now stretch forward to pick it up." The upbringer demonstrated as she talked so children could copy her actions. Next, children were to sit back up and stretch their arms behind themselves and knock the rattles on the floor.

"Now stand up and jump," said the upbringer, changing to a more active exercise. "Hands on your hips while you jump," she instructed.

After the children had jumped in place on both feet for about half a minute, they all walked over to the climber, a wooden ladderlike structure with room for two children per rung. The children climbed up a few rungs while the upbringer stood with her hands held out below their bottoms. She was ready to catch anyone who might fall. Children were cautioned to start at the first rung and never to skip any rungs. One child went all the way to the top rung and was told to come down immediately. The upbringer kept both hands on children's bottoms as they came down. Watching children climb seemed to make her anxious.

After climbing came walking on a balance beam about eight inches off the floor. The upbringer walked alongside each child so that he or she could grab her hand if need be. After getting off the balance beam, children walked on a rug that lay at right angles to it. The rug, which was about five feet long and a foot and a half wide, had one-inch wooden slats running across it at intervals of about one and a half inches. After walking the length of the rug, children returned to run down it. The purpose of these rugs is prophylactic: to prevent fallen arches.

Having completed these exercises, the children were ready for a game of wolf and rabbits. Everyone squatted; when the upbringer put her hands up to her head (to represent wolf ears), the children got up and ran away, laughing. This was repeated three times. Then, finally, it was time to leave. The upbringer told everyone to stand up, stretch to the ceiling, then to the floor. The lesson was over. It was time to dress and return to the classroom.

When I arrived to observe a physical education lesson for 4-year-olds, the children had already undressed to undershirts and underpants. They were marching in single file. The upbringer told them to walk on their tiptoes, then on their heels, and finally on the outer sides of their feet in pigeon-toed fashion. Next they were to run over to a bench that also served as a balance beam, walk across it, step down and over some blocks, and then crawl under a rod held about a foot high.

After everyone had completed this course, the children were told to sit on the bench as if on horseback, one behind the other. Together they held two long poles, one in their left hands and another in their right. The upbringer told them to pretend to be a train as she guided the poles (and the children's arms) forward, back, up, and down. Elena Vavilova's (1981) manual explains that this activity develops arm strength and dexterity.

Next came ball throwing. The children were to stand behind a line and try to throw a ball into a basket about six feet away and about four feet off the floor. After every child had tried making a basket, they marched to the other side of the room as the upbringer called out "one, two, three, one, two, three," and so on.

Finally it was time for a game. Holding a steering wheel, the upbringer pretended to be driving a car. The children pretended to be sparrows flying away from the oncoming car. The "driver" never caught any of the fleeing "sparrows." One child did not want to play. She was allowed to sit on a chair and watch from the sidelines.

I was struck by the frequent praise given children during this lesson. There was never any criticism of children who could not or would not perform as well as others.

SOME CONCLUDING COMMENTS

The reader has surely noticed the match between the general features of lessons described in Chapter 8 and the specific content area goals and implementation practices described in this chapter. Two additional comments are in order. One has to do with the emotional tone of lessons. Despite the heavily didactic nature of upbringer-child interactions during lessons, children seemed to enjoy them. By relating real-world objects and events to the activities and by acting enthusiastic themselves, upbringers were able to maintain children's interest. Moreover, even while looking for "right" answers, most upbringers let "incorrect" ones go with little or no negative feedback.

A second comment has to do with differential treatment of boys and girls. In general, the two sexes have the same opportunities and responsibilities during the day. (Recall from Chapter 7 that both play with blocks and both play with dolls and other items in the housekeeping area. See also Photograph 3 in Chapter 5). Yet in small ways traditional values show through. One upbringer asked the "men" to help her move tables. Another gave boys "somber-colored" flags; girls got lighter ones. A third told 2-year-old boys that during dances it was their role to hold girls' hands firmly. A fourth was glad to see the girls "tender and smiling" in preparation for singing. Observers of Soviet and Russian life (e.g., Gray, 1989; Sanjian, 1991) have written about sexual inequality in Russian homes and work places; it was interesting to see these signs in the microcosm of center care.

Chapter 10

Outside Time

The amount of time allotted to daily outdoor play is evidence of its importance in educators' eyes. Weather permitting, children spend close to four hours each day outside. The Russian idea of "weather permitting," one should add, is not very lenient. Two-year-olds are taken outside to play when the temperature is -15° Centigrade (5° Fahrenheit) or above; older children play outside in even colder weather. (See Chapter 5 for lower limits for all age-groups.)[1] It should be noted that the upbringer has some discretion in amount of time spent outside. On very cold or very hot days, children may be brought outdoors somewhat later than usual and/or brought back indoors somewhat earlier than usual (Bogina & Terekhova, 1987).

The child care personnel I interviewed and the early childhood manuals I have read (e.g., Andreeva& Khukhlaeva, 1986; Bogina& Terekhova, 1987) are entirely consistent with each other in their convictions regarding the benefits of outdoor play. These benefits are believed to include essential opportunities to breathe fresh air, build resistance to weather fluctuations, exercise the cardiovascular system and the large muscles, and learn about the outdoor world. Exposure to fresh air is thought to be so important for children's health that even on very windy or rainy days they are taken outside to play quiet games or listen to stories in the play yard shelters.

Ironically, alongside this adamant belief in the importance of breathing even very cold fresh air is anxiety about children's susceptibility to illness should they become chilled. The solution to this dilemma is to dress them very warmly. There are long-standing jokes about Russian children who are so wrapped up in layers of wool and fur that they can hardly move. A more serious concern is that in a group situation such as in a child care center, the first children to have on all their winter outerwear may become overheated while they wait for the others to finish dressing. Once outside, these children too often become chilled because they are wet from perspiration. Moreover, because of the heavy clothing, even children who go outside immediately after dressing may perspire after a little bit of exercise. As a reaction against this practice, in recent years some pedagogues have taken to encouraging parents and child care workers to let children play outside for a short while each day clad only in their indoor play clothes (e.g., Nikitin & Nikitina, 1990). Less drastic advice is simply to be mindful of overdressing children.

Be that as it may, in the centers in which I observed, dressing to go outside in the winter was a complicated procedure, one that required the help of both the upbringer and the nanny. Both in the morning and in the afternoon, outside time follows lessons. In the case of classrooms of 2-year-olds, the upbringer divides the children into two smaller groups for lessons. She works with the first group while the second group plays under the nanny's supervision. Then, while she conducts the lesson for the second group, the nanny takes the first half, who have just completed their lesson, to the bathroom and then to the dressing room to begin putting on their outerwear. Usually they finish dressing just as the second group of children completes its lesson and arrives in the dressing room. Either the upbringer or the nanny (usually the upbringer) escorts the first group of children outside while the other one stays with the second group of children to help them dress. In either case, once all the children have arrived outside, the upbringer stays with them and the nanny returns indoors.

In the case of groups of children aged 3 and older, all of the children are ready for toileting and dressing at the same time since lessons are conducted with the group as a whole. The nanny and the upbringer together help children with these procedures. (Incidentally, in the centers in which I observed, children were invited but not required to use the bathroom before going outside.) With these age-groups with the younger children, often the upbringer takes the first 10 or so already-dressed children outside so that they will not become overheated. The rest of the children stay with the nanny to finish dressing and go out by themselves or with the nanny when they are ready.

What does dressing entail? Children are taught a definite order in which to put on their outdoor clothing. First, if they are wearing socks, they must take them off and put on tights (boys and girls). Over the tights come either knit leggings or nylon snow pants.

Boots follow. Then sweaters. After sweaters are on, the upbringer or nanny helps many of the girls put on cotton or woolen head scarves. Hats go over the scarves. When I asked why scarves are worn under hats, a nanny told me that the scarves protect children's scalps from the hot, scratchy wool with which many hats are made. Finally, after their hats are on, children put on jackets and then mittens. Parents are asked to be sure each day to put a handkerchief in their children's jacket pockets. These come in very handy for wiping noses.

Children are urged to do as much of the dressing by themselves as they can. The atmosphere in the dressing room often seemed urgent. It was my impression that children were more likely to hear criticism and short directives during dressing time than at other times of the day. Perhaps it was because nannies, who are as a rule less well educated than upbringers, were more involved with children at these times than at others. Perhaps it had something to do with nannies' and upbringers' concern that children hurry so that those who were close to finishing could get outside before they became too hot. Of course it is not easy to supervise 10 to 20 children all putting on winter clothing at once. Small wonder that people become impatient.

One day, for example, I heard a 68-year-old nanny scold a boy, Oleg, who was taking his time, "Rascal! When will you stop being so naughty?" Another boy started to put his sweater on before his tights. "You mean you start with your sweater? What are you supposed to put on first?" When all but one of the children were finally ready to go out, the nanny looked around, asking, "Who is left?" Oleg was left. "Oleg, well, of course," she answered her own question in a sarcastic tone of voice. In another dressing room on another day, a girl began crying. When the upbringer asked her why she was crying, the girl complained that a boy had hit her. "But why haven't you put your boots on as you're supposed to?" asked the upbringer, ignoring what seemed to me to be the more important issue. The focus seemed to be on getting the job of dressing done, and when this didn't go smoothly (as it probably rarely does with children so young), adults became impatient and irritable.

In another center I listened with some dismay as a nanny rebuked a child for being slow and for putting her sweater on backward, "Look, all the other children are ready. What have you been doing? Look at your sweater. Here, take it off and start over." Later I found out that this child was the nanny's own daughter. I wondered if the child had purposely dawdled so as to have some time alone with her mother and if the mother-nanny, on the other hand, had been embarrassed to have her own child be the straggler.

The dressing-room atmosphere is of course not always so hurried and sharp. The same nanny who had criticized Oleg later approached two boys who were yelling at one another in the dressing room and calmly told them, "Alesha, Sasha, it's very noisy." An upbringer who was working without a nanny was most generous with encouragement and praise. "What helpers we have!" she exclaimed glancing at 4-year-olds who were succeeding at getting themselves dressed. "You did it yourself! Smart girl. All grown up!" she told one child. A boy had made a mistake in the prescribed order of dressing; he had put his sweater on before his boots. Smiling, the upbringer asked him, "And where are your boots? Did you forget them?" There was no criticism in her voice. Another child was trying unsuccessfully to button her sweater. The upbringer was solicitous, "You're not getting it? Here, I'll help you." When the child refused help, the upbringer understood. "No? Yourself?" she said, seeing the child's determination to manage by herself. This upbringer maintained her sensitivity to children's abilities and feelings even during the vicissitudes of dressing.

Once outside, children have plenty of time to play as they wish. In fact, even in winter the longest uninterrupted blocks of time for free play occur during outside times. Not only is the amount of time allotted generous; there is also a good array of playthings. Children drew with chalk on the concrete pathways. They squatted in sandboxes, making roadways and cities with the help of buckets, shovels, and thin plywood model buildings. (Children who sat in the sand were warned to squat lest they get too cold or dirty.) Some rode toy cars, tricycles, and bicycles with training wheels. Some twirled hoops. Some threw balls. Some slid down slides, climbed on metal and wooden climbers, and hid in little one-room wooden playhouses. Some swept walkways with child-sized brooms. Some made shapes out of snow. Some strolled with dolls in toy baby carriages. Others played store with dolls, stuffed animals, purses, toy dishes, and cash registers. Small housekeeping items such as these are regularly taken outside at Russian centers.

In addition to time for free play, early childhood manuals (e.g., Andreeva & Khukhlaeva, 1986; Bogina & Terekhova, 1987; Butsinskaia, Vasiukova, & Leskova, 1990) stipulate 10 to 15 minutes of active organized games during outside times. These upbringer-led activities are to be chosen according to the developmental levels and individual interests of the children, the weather (less active games in hot weather), and the time of day (more active games in the morning than in the afternoon).

Circle games are often played. Even more popular, it seemed, were games of chase. A typical one requires children to pretend to be baby birds. They run (fly) around, flapping their arms (wings), then on signal from the upbringer, crouch down, pretending to peck at seeds. The upbringer (mother bird) then claps and exclaims that she sees a wolf, and all the children run to her. Manuals advise upbringers of 2-year-olds and young 3-year-olds to participate fully in these games since children of these ages will lose interest otherwise. As children get older, they can begin to take lead parts. Accordingly, I saw 4- and 5-year-old children play the role of the wolf in chase games; they would try to catch other children as they tried to run by. Older preschoolers were also thought to be less in need of a story theme to maintain interest in games. They might simply play tag, without pretending to be birds and a wolf.

One of the three weekly physical education lessons is held during part of a morning outside time. For these outdoor lessons upbringers might encourage children to practice movements they know are difficult for them, or they might teach outdoor skills such as tricycle or bicycle riding, sledding, skiing down small hills, or (for older children) learning the rudiments of an individual or team sport. Running, jumping, and other movements worked on during indoor physical lessons are also practiced outdoors.

One director explained to me that, in addition to providing for independent free play and the large motor exercise just mentioned, upbringers are responsible for finding time to play with individual children who need extra attention. They are also supposed to do some teaching about nature and the interconnections between nature and human labor.

The teaching that goes on during outside times tends to be informal, not like lessons indoors. In April the upbringer might direct the children's attention to a bird singing nearby. She might then recite a verse about birds in the spring. She might point out some properties of snow and show children how to pack it, how it melts when it gets warm. She might use a disciplinary situation to teach children something about nature. One day I saw a child tearing some leaves off a bush. The upbringer also saw him. "Why are you tearing off leaves? You may look at the twigs but don't break them. If you break off the twigs and buds, then the bushes won't have leaves later.   Don't break anything off bushes any more," she told him.

Teaching about the connections between nature and labor may involve directing children to watch yardmen shoveling snow off walkways, or it may involve requiring children to pick sticks up off the ground themselves.   James Muckle (1990) points out that important goals of Marxist education were to promote understanding of the "dialectical unity" of nature, man, and society and to foster appreciation of the relations between knowledge and action.   Here, in these outside time mini-lessons, we see a practical way to demonstrate these interconnections to young children.

It would be a mistake to convey the impression that upbringers are actively involved with children during most of outside time. Except for the short amounts of time devoted to the required organized games, once-weekly outdoor physical education lessons, and comments about man, nature, and labor, upbringers did what preschool teachers probably do everywhere during outdoor play times: quietly watch children, referee occasional quarrels, wipe runny noses, and chat with upbringers in neighboring play areas. (Recall, from Chapter 5, that the outdoor space of each center is divided so that each group has its own separate play area.)

The busiest upbringer I saw outside was a young woman working with toddlers.   One child had just started walking and kept falling on the slippery snow.   Each time, the upbringer helped her up.   Other children kept taking off their mittens.   The upbringer kept putting them back on.   It was one girl's first day.   She had come for a two-hour period to begin to begin to adjust to the center.   Though she was happy at first, after about 45 minutes she started crying for her mother.   The upbringer sat with the child on her lap for a while, comforting her and assuring her that her mother would soon return.   When she wasn't engaged in these caretaking tasks, this upbringer was showing children how to fill buckets with snow, turn them over, and let the snow fall out in "cakes."

Before children return inside, toys must be put away.   "I'm teaching you to be neat and clean," explained one upbringer as her charges put small toys in a plastic bag.   Larger toys went in plastic laundry baskets.   Some items were left on benches in the shelter to dry.   Neighborhood children who did not attend the centers were allowed to play in the play yards when center children were indoors and during evenings or weekends.   I wondered about theft, but upbringers told me that toys rarely disappeared.

The nanny usually comes outside to help escort children back in after outside time.   If the children are very young (2 or early 3), she brings in only half of them–the ones who were first to go out. These children have about 15 minutes to change back into their indoor clothing before the upbringer brings the other children back in. If the children are older, they all go in together.

As children change back into their indoor clothing, the nanny and upbringer again help children who need it. They also pay attention to children's appearance and cleanliness. Children are reminded to straighten their clothes so that they will look "pretty," to put their outerwear neatly in their closets, and to close their closet doors when they are finished so that the room will be neat.

From the dressing room, children proceed to the bathroom to wash their hands. In the summer, they also wash their legs and feet, and, in at least one center, change their underwear. Without the protection of tights, snow pants, and boots, it is assumed that children's legs, feet, and underwear get dirty when they run around or sit on the ground or in the sandbox.

Lunch follows the morning outside time. If lunch is ready, children go directly from the bathrooms to the tables to eat. If lunch is not yet ready, they engage in quiet free play while they wait, or an upbringer might lead a circle game or read a book.

After afternoon outside times, children engage in free play in the playroom until their parents come or, if they are staying the night, they play until it is time for dinner. It should be noted that in the late afternoon some children are picked up by their parents during outside time. This arrangement works well because the children are already dressed to leave and because the opportunity for upbringer-parent interaction is considerably greater in the play yard than inside. (Recall from Chapter 5 that parents are not allowed in the playrooms.)

Children's health and strength are focal issues for outside time programming. The next chapter describes beliefs and procedures related to eating and sleeping. Health issues will again be of central importance.

NOTE

1. For the sake of comparison, it is interesting to note that an informal check with several preschools in Missouri revealed a low temperature limit of 15° Fahrenheit for outdoor play.

Chapter 11

Meals and Naps

Goal Number 1 of Russian educators and parents is maintaining and improving children's health. An article on school reform contains one teacher's lament, "We live in a time of sick children" (, 1990, p. 6). Many times I heard similar words. Even prior to perestroika and glasnost', Russia and the Soviet Union had suffered a long history of difficult health conditions (Ransel, 1991; Smith, 1976). Recent social and economic changes have exacerbated these problems. During the last few years epidemics of dysentery, diphtheria, polio, tuberculosis, hepatitis, and influenza have been linked to the high cost of vaccinations, poor food handling procedures by private vendors, and the unavailability and/or prohibitive cost of fresh fruits, vegetables, milk products, and meat. Contributing to people's anxiety about illness is the fact that the quality of medical care has also experienced a significant decline ("Amid Economic," 1992; "Gosstandart," 1993).

Against this backdrop, the considerable energy that goes into guarding children from germs and strengthening their resistance to illness is understandable. Some information on health-related procedures has been presented in Chapters 3, 5, 6, and 10. The present chapter describes in detail policies and practices specific to meals and naps—times of the day when health concerns are paramount. Unless otherwise indicated, the information I present is taken from my observations and interviews and from two books for child care personnel—one on the daily routine (Bogina & Terekhova, 1987), and one on preparing and serving meals (Alekseeva, Druzhinina, & Ladodo, 1990).

MENUS

Children who stay at the center for a typical 9- or 10- hour day
are fed breakfast, lunch, and an afternoon snack. Children who stay
past 6:15 in the evening are also served dinner. In 1984 the USSR
Ministry of Health, in consultation with the USSR Ministry of
Education, published new nutritional standards. Children's ages and
the number of hours they spend at the center were considered in
determining the number of calories and the protein, fat,
carbohydrate, and vitamin content required in each meal. Sample
menus took into account seasonal availability of foods and cultural
traditions and preferences. These guidelines are still in place.

Breakfast

The guidelines stipulate that breakfast should provide 25% of
the preschooler's daily caloric intake. My notes from one breakfast
show children eating kasha (buckwheat groats) cooked in milk and
mixed with butter and sugar, white bread topped with butter and
cheese, and "coffee" (a drink made from acorns, cereal grains, or
chicory) sweetened with sugar and milk. The sample menus
recommend adding dried fruits to the kasha, but these were
unavailable on the days I observed. Toward the end of my visit,
much to directors' distress, food deliveries were falling short in
terms of fruits and vegetables.

On other days kasha, oatmeal, macaroni and cheese, potato or
cottage cheese pudding, an omelette, a fish dish, or hot dogs might
appear on the breakfast table. All except macaroni and cheese are
generally accompanied by rice, potatoes, apple or pumpkin pieces,
or dried fruit. Bread and butter are available for breakfast daily, as
is a cup of either "coffee" or tea with milk and sugar.

Lunch

The noontime meal, which I will call lunch although it might be
more accurate to call it dinner, is a three-course affair. The main
meal of the day, it is supposed to provide approximately 40% of
children's daily caloric intake.

The first lunch course is always soup (usually *borshch* or *shchi*)
made with either fish or meat stock and vegetables (typically
cabbage and beets) or with peas and macaroni. Soup is a staple in

the Russian diet, and a bowl of it each day is considered essential for good health and proper digestion. Bread is always served with soup.

The second lunch course includes a fish, chicken, or beef patty; a starch, such as mashed potatoes, noodles, or rice, mixed cooked or raw vegetables–carrots, cabbage, beets, peas, and/or cucumbers; and fruit, such as apples or oranges. This is the last time of the day when meat may be served. It is believed that meat requires more digestive juices and takes longer to digest than do other foods; therefore it should be eaten early in the day rather than close to bedtime.

Though fresh fruit is preferred, at the time of my visit it was in short supply, and the third lunch course was always stewed fruit compote. Ascorbic acid drops (Vitamin C) were added to this compote. Children also received supplementary multivitamin pills. A nurse told me that extra vitamins are given in the spring because fresh fruits and vegetables are particularly scarce at that time.

Afternoon Snack

The afternoon snack makes up 15% of the daily caloric intake. It always includes milk or a milk-based drink such as kefir (a yogurt-like drink) sweetened with sugar, a baked item such as a roll, pancake, pastry, or cottage cheese pudding, and, if available, a piece of fruit such as an orange half.

Dinner

Dinner is intended to provide 20% of children's daily caloric intake. Most children eat dinner at home, but for those who stay at the center, dinner consists of a milk drink (milk, kefir, or tea with milk), a piece of bread, and two of the following: fruit, a vegetable dish, and/or a cottage cheese pudding. Dinner is thus a light meal–a supper, actually–and, as mentioned, includes neither meat nor fish.

Foods That May Not Be Served

In each center, the nurse is responsible for planning meals, overseeing the ordering of foodstuffs, and making sure that cooks, nannies, and upbringers adhere to the rules of proper hygiene when preparing and serving meals. Because of fear of food poisoning, certain foods are never served, and others are cooked more stringently than in the United States. Cream, mayonnaise, and mushrooms may not be used in cooking. Dishes such as macaroni with ground meat, meat wrapped in pancakes, meat in gel, meat patés, fish patties, and meat or fish fried in animal fat are forbidden because they must be reheated and/or they spoil easily. For the same reasons, no commercially pre-cooked foods are permitted. Canned foods, milk, and water must be boiled, and milk products such as cottage cheese and sour cream must have been heated before they are served. Fresh fruit may be served raw, although this may change since, as a pediatrician told me, there is growing concern about fruit-borne dysentery.

FOCUS ON HABITS AND MANNERS

Considerable effort goes into making sure that children eat. In this regard Bogina and Terekhova (1987), and Alla Alekseeva, Lidia Druzhinina, and Kaleriia Ladodo (1990) emphasize the importance of serving meals at the same times each day (to develop and maintain a time-sensitive "appetite reflex"). They also stress the need for comfortable and attractive table settings, food that is pleasing in appearance and smell, and a calm, unhurried atmosphere. Both sets of authors urge upbringers to refrain from pressuring children to eat lest they develop negative reactions to certain foods. As will become clear below, in every center my observations indicated adherence to set schedules and the "aesthetics of eating," but not to the notion of a relaxed mealtime atmosphere.

While issues related to nutrition are paramount in the planning and execution of mealtimes, teaching children good hygiene habits and polite table manners is also considered of great importance. Before meals, children wash their hands with soap and dry them on their personal towels. During meals they are expected to keep their heads bent over their plates so their clothing will stay clean, to chew quietly with their mouths closed (no slurping and no talking), to hold their spoons or forks in their right hands and, while eating soup, a piece of bread in their left hands (unless they are known to be left-handed, in which case the pattern is reversed). The bread may be eaten; it is also used as a "helper" for pushing food onto spoons. According to Alekseeva, Druzhinina, and Ladodo (1990), forks should be introduced when children are 3 years old. One director, however, told me that forks are not used until children are 4; until that time they use only spoons. (This director was upset because her *yasli* was being converted to accommodate children up to the age of 6, but she could find no forks to buy.)

The adults in the classroom (the nanny and either one or two upbringers, depending on when the second-shift upbringer arrives) take turns eating separately in the serving area while the children eat, or they wait until the children are asleep. They do not sit with the children during meals; their role is to bring children their portions and to monitor their eating. The only food children take for themselves is bread from a small basket in the middle of each table. At lunchtime, as individual children finish a course, the upbringer and nanny take their plates away and bring them the next course. Thus after a few minutes different children sitting at the same table may be eating different courses.

Toward the end of the meal, when most children have been served their compote, the nanny begins washing dishes. Usually this task is done in the classroom or in a small adjacent room. If any of the children in the group has an infectious illness, dishes are to be soaked for 30 minutes in a chlorine solution before being rinsed with very hot water. All dishes are air dried. (None of the centers have automatic dishwashers.)

Mealtime *dezhurstvo*, in which children take turns helping the nanny set tables and serve food, is practiced in some centers. Bogina and Terekhova (1987), however, note that too often children serving this role are sent inside alone 10 or 15 minutes before the end of outside time. No one monitors them as they wash up in preparation for their jobs. Not surprisingly, sanitation suffers. Perhaps for this reason I never saw mealtime *dezhurstvo* in the centers I visited.

Not only is no conversation among children permitted during mealtimes. Back-and-forth conversation between adults and children is also rare; when it occurs, it is invariably centered on eating. I heard three different reasons for the prohibition against talking: it prevents children from choking; it teaches politeness (no talking with a full mouth); and it keeps mealtimes from lasting too long.

This is not to imply, however, that upbringers and nannies are silent. Some upbringers wish children "good appetites" as they start the meal. Though Alekseeva, Druzhinina, & Ladodo, (1990) warn against hurrying children or calling attention to how quickly or slowly they are eating, in fact I found that both occur quite regularly. Upbringers and nannies seemed very much interested in having children eat all that they have been served, eat quickly, and eat politely.   There were many comments praising fast eaters and coaxing slow ones.   Children who seemed uninterested in eating were spoon-fed even as they were scolded for not eating independently (see Photograph 16).

At the meal's end, children may not get up from the table until they have finished chewing. After finishing their fruit compote (the last course), they are to wipe their mouths and hands with a napkin, turn to face an upbringer or nanny to say thank you, and take their cups and napkins to the serving area. In some groups they then take their chairs either to the side of the room or to the bedroom. In other groups they do this a bit later, when it is time to prepare for naps.   They will use these chairs shortly when they undress.   Children need not wait for the whole group to finish eating before they leave the table, and they may play quietly with toys of their own choosing until it is time to prepare for nap time.

The following transcript of a mealtime is illustrative. It is based on my notes taken during lunch one day and is representative of the mealtimes I observed. The reader will note that the climate was mixed; in an atmosphere of overall warmth, approval for compliance and shaming of noncompliance conveyed clear messages about proper behavior.

Usually I observed alone, but this time I was accompanied by the center nurse and a researcher from the Institute for Preschool Education. The nurse, of course, was an integral part of the center system.   As far as I could tell, she approved of the way the upbringer and nanny handled mealtime issues.   The researcher had traveled in the West and wished to see more opportunities for children to express their personal preferences; she was not altogether comfortable with the scene she was observing. Perhaps the presence of an American onlooker exacerbated this feeling.

As children finished taking off their outerwear and putting on their indoor shoes, they proceeded to the bathroom to wash up for lunch. The upbringer supervised as children washed their hands with soap. Some washed their faces also, but this was not required. The upbringer combed the hair of girls whose hair had been messed up by their scarves or hats. Afterward the girls were told to hang their combs back up "prettily." The upbringer used a kindly, singsong voice as she directed children.

Lunch was ready, so the children went directly to the tables as they left the bathroom. The first course was a piece of bread and *borshch* made of beets and cabbage with a dollop of sour cream. The bread was already on the table; as each child sat down, the nanny or upbringer brought over his or her soup. Bibs were put on a few children who had not yet mastered the art of eating neatly. Not wanting a bib, one girl promised to eat neatly. The upbringer agreed to let her try.

Warmly, cheerfully, the upbringer conveyed her enthusiasm about the meal. There were also some rules to review: "Now look, children. Ekaterina Ivanovna [the nanny] has set the tables so nicely! What did she give us? Soup. Spoons. Which hand holds the spoon? The right one. Show me your right hand." All but three children raised their right hands. "Masha and Sasha and Dima don't know. Everyone take your spoon in your *right* hand. Everyone sit straight. You know the saying: 'When I eat I am deaf and dumb.' Children should eat quietly, their heads bowed over their plates so their clothes will stay clean."

As required, the children ate silently. During most of the mealtime the only sounds were the occasional clinking of spoons on china and the urgings of the nanny and upbringer.

"What are we eating?" asked the upbringer.

"Soup," answered the children.

"Yes. Is the soup tasty?"

"Yes," answered some children.

"Good. Pleasant appetites," the upbringer wished them.

"Thank you," replied the children.

The instructions and reminders continued: "Sit nicely at the table. Dima, you're not left-handed." Spotting a child who was holding her spoon correctly, the upbringer pointed her out as an example, "See, now Masha is holding her spoon the right way. Who knows how to hold a spoon?"

"They're OK. Let them be," interjected the researcher sitting next to me. I couldn't tell if the upbringer heard her.

"Eat, eat, cute little rabbits," the upbringer and nanny coaxed as they surveyed the room. "Misha, how are you eating? How do we tip our bowls? Help with the cute little bread. Lean over your bowl. Scoot your chair up to the table. Eat, eat, cute little children. Eat neatly. Eat, eat. Masha, eat some soup with your bread. Ania, take some cute little bread. Everyone is eating neatly, not spilling. Sasha is eating neatly. Don't smack your lips. Lilia, the other children are about to win. Finish quickly."

One child said she didn't want any more *borshch*. She happened to be sitting at the table closest to the little group of observers. "Have two more spoonfuls and that will be enough," the researcher allowed.

The upbringer patted some children's heads affectionately. "Eat quickly, cute little children. Sasha is the first to finish. Good for you! Alesha, eat quickly! So, Sasha has eaten. Roma is catching up. Sasha and Roma are big. The soup is good for you. Sasha and Roma will grow up to be strong."

The upbringer thought Masha might hurry up if she knew that the nanny was too busy at the moment to spoon-feed her. "Masha, eat quickly. No one is going to [spoon-]feed you. Grandmother [the nanny] is busy eating her own lunch."

Finally all but Lilia and Masha had finished their *borshch*. "Lilia, look. Almost everyone ate faster than you," the upbringer accused. Pulling over a chair, the nanny, who had just finished eating her own meal, proceeded to spoon-feed Lilia. "Lilia, what's with you? Were you waiting for Grandmother? It's shameful. You are big, yet you ate poorly." The nanny spoke in sad rather than angry tones. After she finished feeding Lilia, she did the same for Masha. (Photograph 16 shows a spoon-feeding episode.)

The nurse was upset by this scene, but for a different reason than I might have been. When I whispered to her that Lilia would most likely eat on her own if not fed a time or two, she shrugged her shoulders skeptically. She was upset that the child wouldn't eat on her own but was sure that the nanny was doing the right thing. She disagreed with me that the child either really wasn't hungry or needed to learn that the alternative to feeding herself was simply not eating.

As children finished their *borshch*, their bowls were taken away and they were given a plate with a meatball and mashed potatoes. Children were offered sauce for their meatballs; those who didn't want it didn't have to have any. On the side there was a salad of shredded carrots.

One girl asked another a question. "Who is talking? Eat!" the upbringer brought her back to the task at hand.

At this point the music upbringer walked in. She greeted the group cheerfully: "Hello, cute little children! Pleasant appetites!" "Hello, thank you," some children answered.

"Lena, you don't want to eat? Too lazy?" the upbringer wanted to make sure that children continued eating. She had particularly sharp words for Nadia: "I think Nadia isn't sitting prettily at the table. You're the biggest one, and yet you have a finger in your mouth. I don't like it at all. Sit prettily. Sit straight. Bow only your head." Another child was urged on in warmer tones: "Anya, eat some more, my golden one."

Some children had finished their second course. One of them came in for extravagant praise: "What a smart boy! Your plate is clean. You ate everything. You are so big! If you eat everything on your plate, you'll grow up to be big and healthy and strong."

Another boy with a clean plate wanted to be noticed too: "Look how big I am!"

Another claimed that he was faster than another. "I beat him!" The upbringer complimented him, "Good for you! You are all grown up!"

Children who did not want to eat everything on their plates, though not forced to eat more, were made to feel ashamed. One who left some potatoes on his plate was asked if he always eats so poorly. Others who either ate slowly or did not clean off their plates were asked if they were still "little." The exception was a child who started coughing; he was told to take his time.

Children who did eat everything that had been served them were offered seconds, but there was no pressure to accept. Those who were finished with the second course were served their fruit compote. The nanny now began washing dishes. As children finished the compote, they wiped their mouths with their napkins, stood up, pushed their chairs in under the table, thanked the nanny or the upbringer for the meal, carried their cups to a bench near the sink where the nanny was washing dishes, and threw their napkins into a nearby trash can. Children who forgot to help clear the table, push in their chairs, or say thank you were cheerfully reminded to return to their tables to do so.

Of course some children were faster than others at reaching this point. As with the first and second courses, there was praise for those who finished first. The child who was the very first to finish everything came in for special attention, "There! Mishka, good for you! You ate the fastest!" the upbringer exclaimed. The second child to finish also received enthusiastic praise: "Good for you! You're outstanding!" When, despite his wonderful appetite, he left the table without thanking anyone and without pushing in his chair, the upbringer called him back, "You've eaten? What are you supposed to say?" The child remembered, "Thank you." "You're welcome," responded the upbringer. "Push in your cute little chair." After he had done so, she had one more instruction, "Tuck your shirt in and you may play." Children who were not yet finished with their second course were urged to do so quickly. "Sasha, look. The other children have already eaten and gone to play."

The children who were finished eating were allowed to play quietly. A boy who wanted to play with the large riding cars was told to find something else to do; upbringers want children to stay calm so that they will be ready for nap time. They also do not want children who are still eating to be distracted. (The rules are more relaxed at snack time, a less important meal; noisy play is permitted then while fast eaters wait for others to finish.)

Why do upbringers and nannies do so much coaxing during mealtimes? At first I thought it was mostly due to pressure to keep to the daily schedule, to get children to bed on time. There is more to it, though. I had some insight one day from a nanny. It was snack time. "Eat, eat," she urged a child. "I don't want to," replied the child. "What do you mean you don't want to? Eat!" returned the nanny. Then, turning to me, she explained, "We have good children. But some of them eat poorly. You have to talk them into eating. Well, what can we do? Children are children." I had

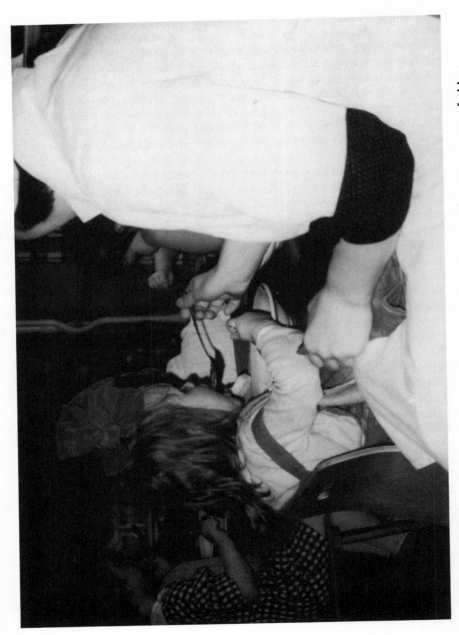

Photograph 16. Lilia did not seem interested in eating her soup, so the nanny spoon-fed her.

heard similar comments before and was to hear more later. These child care providers believe that they, not children, should regulate children's eating. Children might not eat enough on their own. Nutrition is too serious to be left to the whims of children's appetites.

PREPARING FOR NAP TIME

The exact procedures used in preparation for naps differs from center to center. In one center, for example, children bring chairs from the tables to form a semicircle around the upbringer. She reads them a story. The intent, of course, is to create a calm atmosphere, predisposing the children to sleep. In another center the upbringer reads a story aloud after the children are in their beds. In yet other centers preparation for naps includes a procedure designed to toughen children against the cold. (Two such procedures are described below.)

Undressing

In all centers, before undressing children take their chairs from the tables and put them in a straight line, either at one end of the playroom or in front of their beds in the bedroom. In many centers this is part of the ritual that follows the completion of lunch. After they have added their chairs to the line, they may play for a short while. When it is time to undress, they take off all of their clothing except for undershirts and underpants. Shoes are left under the chairs and other clothing on the chairs. They will remain there while the children sleep.

Upbringers urge children to undress quickly and hang their clothes neatly on the chairs. One day I wrote down the following words addressed to 3-year-olds: "We hang everything neatly on the cute little chairs. Who was playing with the construction set? Put it away. Hang things neatly. Cute little shorts. Cute little tights. Dima, should I help you or can you unbutton your shirt yourself? Oi! Sasha unbuttoned his shirt by himself! Good for you!"

Toughening

In some centers toughening, or training of resistance to the cold, comes next. Toughening has been a custom for generations in Russia and Scandinavia (Bronfenbrenner, 1970b; Dunn, 1974); directors decide whether or not and to what extent to practice it in their centers. In one center the toughening procedure involved having the children walk barefoot and clad in only undershirts and underpants over three rugs, each about 5 feet by 1 1/2 feet and arranged perpendicularly to one another (i.e., in a square with one side missing). The middle rug was dry; the other two had been dipped in cold water. As children left their chairs where they had undressed, they walked on a cold, wet rug, then on the dry one, then on the other cold, wet one. Then they returned to their chairs to put their shoes on and proceed to the bedroom and to bed. (Shoes must be worn on the floor lest feet get dirty.)

In another center the procedure was more elaborate, involving a sequence called contrast pouring. Part of this procedure is shown in Photograph 17. After undressing, the children sat down one at a time on a chair facing the nanny. The nanny poured water over the child's legs, first cold water (about 15° Centigrade, or 59° Fahrenheit), then warm water (about 36° Centigrade, or 96.8° Fahrenheit). This was repeated three times. The water had been prepared earlier and checked with a thermometer. The warm water was in a pail to the nanny's right; the cold water was in a pail to her left. Each time she scooped water out of the pails with a small pot. Under the child's legs was a third pail; water poured off the child's legs into it. After this procedure, the nanny dried the child's legs with a fresh rough towel. She called this a "massage." Then the child stood up and walked across a long rug with slats in it. The purpose of this was to prevent flat feet. The next stop was bed.

One director, when I asked her if her upbringers practice toughening, replied that they do not, except to open the windows in the bedroom to air it out and bring in fresh air before children come in to lie down. She said that sometimes children walk barefoot for a while, but I saw this only when children went from the bedroom to the bathroom and back in their bare feet.

Does toughening really work? No one knows, but I recently read with interest a report on a relevant study by the Thrombosis Research Institute in England. Adult volunteers who took daily cold baths had higher levels of white blood cells than they had had

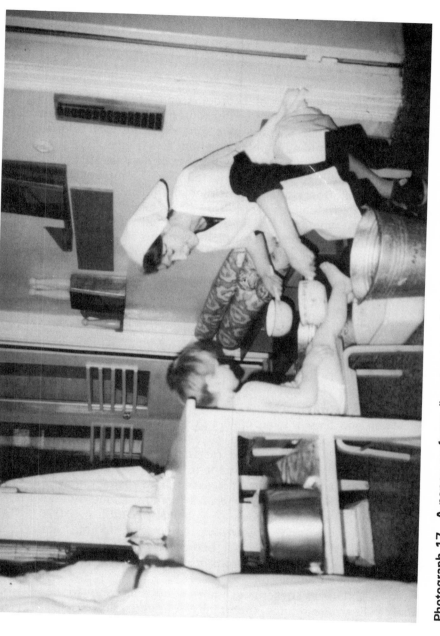

Photograph 17. A nanny performs "contrast pouring" to train resistance to the cold.

before they started the regimen ("Research Throws," 1993). White blood cells help fight colds and influenza.

IN BED

Recall the description of bedrooms and beds in Chapter 5. To cut down on interaction between children during nap times, bedding is arranged so that children sleep in a head-to-foot arrangement; each child's head is next to his neighbor's feet (see Photograph 7 in Chapter 5). In some centers, upbringers or nannies tuck children in and expect them to be quiet and fall asleep right away. In other centers more effort is made to help children relax. Some upbringers read stories; the children listen from their beds. I watched as one upbringer, a woman with a great store of memorized children's poetry, walked around quietly reciting verses about sleep. As she moved around, she tucked several children in with an affectionate pat, wordlessly moved the legs of a child who was bothering his neighbor, and whispered to wakeful children to close their eyes.

All children are required to lie down and remain quiet for the two-hour nap period, even if they are not tired. Several times I peeked in and saw children lying in bed silently but with their eyes wide open.

GETTING UP

When nap time is over, children use the bathrooms and put their clothes back on. Five- and 6-year-olds also make their beds. Upbringers and nannies are to resist the impulse to straighten the beds themselves. "It is important to remember that the child is an individual requiring respect. It is essential to respect his work. The child loses interest in work when his work is redone by adults right before his eyes" (Kutsakova & Pushnina, 1986, p. 101). One upbringer of 5- and 6-year-olds apologized to me about the appearance of the beds in her bedroom. The children had made them and she had refrained from perfecting their efforts. I thought the beds looked wonderful.

In addition to describing meal- and nap-time routines, this chapter has raised some important issues regarding discipline. The next chapter is devoted to a discussion of actual and recommended disciplinary practices.

Chapter 12

Discipline

The tidiness of the playrooms and the cheerful, well-mannered demeanor of most of the children I observed are clearly documented in the slides I took in Moscow. "How do they keep the room so neat?" "How do they get 2-year-olds to sit still for 10 minutes?" I hear questions such as these every time I show my slides to American early childhood educators. This chapter is a discussion of techniques upbringers use to encourage desired behavior in children. Though many of these techniques have been mentioned in conjunction with other issues (particularly in Chapters 4 and 7 through 11), the topic is important enough to merit a separate, focused view. Like other chapters, this chapter juxtaposes recommendations from the Russian early childhood literature with actual recent practice as I saw it.

While it is safe to say that most parents and teachers the world over wish to see children behaving in accordance with cultural norms, Soviet educators had extra stimulus for wanting to see well-behaved children. The pedagogical literature reminded them that the whole of society depended on their work. It was the responsibility of parents and teachers to raise citizens who would benefit rather than burden society (Makarenko, 1967/1937; Peterina, 1986). At the preschool level it was "necessary always to bring to the child's awareness that the work he has done [keeping things neat and orderly] is necessary not only for him, but also for his peers, for other children, for adults. This provides the opportunity to underline one more time the societal value of work" (Kutsakova & Pushnina, 1986, p. 93).

PREVENTION OF MISBEHAVIOR

The Russian early childhood literature on guidance, like its American counterpart, advocates preventing misbehavior through "positive" rather than punitive means. Kutsakova and Pushnina (1986) tell upbringers that "You shouldn't look too long and angrily for the child at fault, grumbling [threats such as] 'I'll hide all the toys if you break them.' It's more effective to approach children with a request since they will react to it more willingly" (p. 94). Peterina (1986) warns that criticism and punishment often have an effect opposite to that intended because they bring out "negative emotions" in children toward the upbringer, toward rules, and toward themselves. Moreover, other children may perceive the punished child as a "bad" child and develop negative attitudes toward him or her. Along the same lines, Nemov (1990), a psychologist, argues that educators should persuade children, not punish or threaten them. When dealing with misbehavior, they should be careful not to moralize and not to make judgments based on prejudices about the involved children.

How does the upbringer "persuade" children to comply with the rules of good behavior? The following sections provide details on recommended strategies. The first involves creating a climate of warmth and mutual positive regard.

Creating a Calm, Warm, and Caring Atmosphere

According to early childhood manuals and upbringers' and directors' comments to me, the first and foremost task of the upbringer is to foster a calm, positive atmosphere in her group, one in which the children feel that she is fond of them and respects them. To create this kind of climate she must be even-tempered, fair, kind, and tactful.

Calm is necessary so that the child's nervous system is not overly taxed (Bogina & Terekhova, 1987). Fairness is important, so that no child feels neglected or rejected in favor of others. One upbringer told me, "You have to live in peace with *all* the children. You shouldn't pick at any one of them."

Kindness and tact are required for several reasons. First, children are more willing to trust and obey an adult who shows consideration, understanding, and affection for them. Second, the upbringer who is kind and tactful serves as a model of these important qualities. Being prone to imitation, young children are very susceptible to example, particularly from an adult whom they like (Peterina, 1986). Third, a tactful upbringer is respectful of young children's striving for independence and does not stifle their initiative (Kutsakova & Pushnina, 1986).

All playrooms have dolls and stuffed toy animals, and some have nature corners with live animals (fish, birds, hamsters, etc.). These also play a role in creating a climate of kindness. It is assumed that children will generalize from gentle behavior with these toys and pets to concern for real animals and people. Kutsakova and Pushnina (1986) quote an upbringer who demonstrated the required attitude as she fed a caged bird: "Good and pretty bird, you are so little, we all love you, and now we will pour you some water, give you some seeds, so that you will always sing your songs for us" (p. 85). In Chapter 9 of this book there are two relevant examples from my observations. In the language and science lesson for 2-year-olds, the upbringer asked the children to lower their voices and refrain from touching the bird cage lest they scare the parakeet. In the second music lesson example, the upbringer insisted that a child hold a toy cat in such a way as to make it comfortable.

Occasionally children may laugh when another child or an adult gets hurt; Kononova (1989) writes that the upbringer must take advantage of such moments to teach concern for others. She must explain, for example, that it is inappropriate to laugh when a child falls. Reading this essay, I was reminded of an incident during one music lesson I observed. The upbringer, who was practicing a dance with her 4-year-olds, suddenly tripped over a chair and fell to the floor. Within a second or so she was laughing at herself. The children also laughed, some heartily. The music upbringer was not at all pleased with the children's reaction. She treated them to a short lecture on why they should not laugh at accidents. "Don't laugh, children. She could have hurt herself. Instead of laughing, you should ask her if she is OK."

Providing Age-Appropriate Equipment and Curricula

The equipment and curriculum are also considered key elements in the prevention of misbehavior. Bogina and Terekhova (1987) and Peterina (1986) stress the importance of toys that can accommodate more than one child at a time (e.g., a large enough toy stove so that two children can cook together) and sufficient numbers of smaller toys so that sharing problems are reduced. Furniture and play materials should be aesthetically pleasing, comfortable, and easy to manipulate so that children will want to use them and take good care of them. To encourage respect for adults, there should be dramatic play props (e.g., brooms, barbershop equipment, etc.) for acting out workers' roles.

Both manuals carry messages about the importance of developmentally appropriate activities and opportunities for movement. In their absence, children will be frustrated and bored, and frustration and boredom are ingredients for disruptive behavior. Peterina (1986) also recommends some variety in the daily routine so that children do not become inflexible.

A good example of flexibility and attention to children's needs occurred one day right before nap time. The children had eaten lunch and had arranged their chairs in a semicircle so that they could listen to their upbringer read a book. She had thought the story would calm them down for sleep. Instead, a girl stood up on her chair to demonstrate how big she was. Then, one by one, other children began to follow suit. The upbringer calmly asked them to sit down. They complied, but a few were still fidgety. "This book doesn't interest you?" the upbringer asked. "No," answered several children. A few others said they wanted to hear it. "Let's go along with the children who are too tired to listen. Let's go to bed," the upbringer decided without criticizing anyone. It was obvious that too many children were too tired to listen or even to allow others to listen. I was impressed with the good cheer with which this upbringer handled this situation. She realized that her attempt to read at this time was inappropriate and, without blaming anyone, altered her plans to better fit the needs of the children.

Using Literature, Dolls, Puppets, and Songs

Modeling kindness, maintaining a developmentally appropriate curriculum, and providing attractive equipment conducive to both sharing and individual play are all, in a sense, indirect, behind-the-scenes disciplinary strategies. More direct means are also advocated. One involves the use of stories, songs, and short dramatizations that communicate standards of correct behavior. Upbringers read stories to children with clear messages about the importance of politeness, obedience, helpfulness, and showing respect for adults (especially for workers, mothers, and grandmothers). Some years ago, stories with patriotic themes were popular, but these were not in evidence when I observed in 1991.

Upbringers may put on short plays using puppets, dolls, or stuffed animals. Educators recommend using these to demonstrate correct behavior and to stimulate discussion about incorrect behavior. As an example of the latter, Peterina (1986) recommends a short play about a naughty kitten who burns his paws when he doesn't listen to his mother's warnings.

Stories and plays may be followed by activities requiring children to act out the behavior being taught. Peterina (1986) gives an example of a politeness lesson: the upbringer acted out a scene with *matreshki* (nested dolls). Each time she opened a doll to take out the next smaller one, the bigger dolls said hello and bowed slightly to the new one. After this demonstration on proper greeting behavior was over, children were given *matreshki* and told to copy the upbringer's example.

Practicing and Repeating Good Habits

Explaining and demonstrating a desired behavior are not enough. Children must practice these behaviors over and over until they become habits. Peterina (1986) reminds upbringers that they should first make sure that new behaviors they wish to instill are age appropriate and attractive in some way. Then, tactfully, without forcing, they should have the children perform the behaviors over and over until they have become automatic. The most obvious examples involve routine behaviors such as pushing one's chair under the table upon getting up, putting clothing on in the proper order, washing hands before eating, and so on.

Giving Children Responsibility

One of the brilliant (and gutsy) strategies used by Anton Makarenko with delinquent adolescents was to honor them by entrusting them with significant responsibilities. He reasoned that in so doing he was "co-opting" them, getting them on his side (Makarenko, 1951/1935). Though early childhood educators work mostly with children without serious behavior problems, they have adopted Makarenko's notion that children must be given meaningful work. Starting in some centers when they are about 3 1/2 years old, children are assigned to *dezhurstvo*, or "duty." While on *dezhurstvo*, they are in charge of a job such as setting the table or cleaning up after a lesson. At first these jobs are those that take no more than 10 minutes; as children get older, the tasks become more involved.   It is considered an honor to be assigned to *dezhurstvo* and, because there is often only minimal adult supervision, children are made to feel that they are really doing important work themselves.   Kutsakova and Pushnina (1986) explain that engagement of children in work is vital to the development of respect for adult roles.   With that respect will come willingness to comply with adults' standards and expectations.   Photograph 18 shows a boy and a girl performing their *dezhurstvo*, putting art supplies away after a lesson.   The expressions on their faces suggest that they take the job seriously and find satisfaction in it.

Using Play Form

In Chapter 7, I noted that upbringers often use pretend play to motivate children to clean up (e.g., children who need to put toy cars away are asked to "park" them "in the garage").   In Chapter 8 I showed how pretend is used to motivate children to participate in lessons.   Kutsakova and Pushnina (1986) explain that the effectiveness of play form grows from the fact that it "allows the upbringer, on the one hand to hide her pedagogical position and, on the other hand, to more actively influence the child" (p. 86).

Play form is used to make routine events interesting for children. Two examples stand out.   One upbringer regularly asked children to form a "bubble" when she wanted them to get in a circle for a group game.   When, after a few minutes the children would bunch up again, she would exclaim, "Oh, our bubble is getting too small again!"   Children would then know to spread out.

A more involved example was part of one group's daily toileting procedure before naps.   After all of the children had undressed to underpants, undershirts, and sandals, they would form a line, each holding on to the bottom of the undershirt of the child ahead of him or her. (See Photograph 19).   Noisily, making "choo-choo" sounds and laughing, the line would proceed to the bathroom.   The upbringer would address behavior problems within the train theme. For example, while they were waiting for all the children to "hook up," one child complained that another was pulling too hard on his undershirt.   "Don't pull.   What will happen if you do?" the upbringer asked the perpetrator.   "The train will have an accident," he replied. "Yes, an accident," the upbringer agreed.   When the "train" started moving before the last child had joined it, the upbringer stopped it: "Don't go yet.   The light is red."   Once in the bathroom, the

Photograph 18. Two children fulfill their *dezhurstvo*, putting art supplies away after a lesson. The boy seated at the table did not complete his project during the lesson and must work on it until he has finished it. The rest of the children are dressing to go outside.

Photograph 19. Children form a train to make the trip from the bedroom to the bathroom.

children would wait for each other to finish before forming the train again to return, laughing, to the bedroom.

Praising Good Behavior

Every Soviet/Russian early childhood manual that I have read advocates generous use of praise for good behavior; the reader has seen numerous examples of praise in previous chapters. Indeed I was quite struck with the amount of praise children heard each day in the centers I visited; I had a strong sense that it was used there more frequently than in the American centers in which I had observed.

Praise is understood by Russian pedagogues to be a powerful stimulus for future effort, both for the child whose good behavior is being acknowledged and for other children who see how to win adult approval. Accordingly, of 63 upbringers who responded to my questionnaire, 58 (92%) agreed with the statement "I think it's better to praise a child when he is good; it gets better results than punishing him when he misbehaves. (Four–6%–were not sure and one–2%–disagreed.) Peterina (1986) suggests that upbringers first praise children for compliance regardless of how well they perform, but that gradually they raise their standards so that only high quality work earns praise.

Though praise usually follows desirable behavior, it may also be used beforehand to set up positive expectations. Kutsakova and Pushnina (1986) suggest, for example, that an upbringer can succeed in getting a child to clean up by first praising her: "Our Olia is a good housekeeper. Now she is going to pick all the rags up off the floor, fold them, and put them away in the closet. It will be clean and neat in her home" (p. 85). The upbringer in this example was probably hoping that her words would motivate not only Olia. Other children might also want to clean up so that they too could be thought of as "good housekeepers."

This example illustrates a point not made in the Russian manuals. Most of the examples in these books, and most of those I heard during my observations, involved what American psychologists and educators have called "praise" as opposed to "encouragement" (e.g., Dinkmeyer, McKay, & Dinkmeyer, 1980). The distinction is a subtle one, but one that many consider important. In the first case, praise of the child, the adult offers accolades such as those the reader has seen in previous chapters: "smart boy," "good for you," "my golden one," "you are outstanding," "you are all grown up," "you are so big." In the case of "encouragement," the child hears words such as "good job," "your drawing is beautiful," etc.   Dinkmeyer, McKay, and Dinkmeyer worry that praise fosters dependence on adult approval and that it can backfire in terms of children's self-confidence on those occasions when their work is unsatisfactory. Are they now no longer "good" or "big" or "golden" children? Encouragement, on the other hand, is focused on the work rather than on the child and thus carries with it less emotional baggage.

When Americans ask why it is that Russian children seem more manageable than American children, even in the face of an adult to child ratio of 1:20, I think of praise as playing a significant role. Since praise signifies adult approval, in settings where it is doled out generously, its absence (when the child has been noncompliant) probably carries great impact.   Wanting to continue to be seen as "good" by the adult, the child will try to conform to her wishes. Though the Russian early childhood literature does not explicitly recognize this connection, upbringers are made aware that children will be more likely to behave correctly if they have positive feelings for adults (e.g., Peterina, 1986).   Praise is one way to win those positive feelings while at the same giving clear messages about which behaviors are acceptable and which are not.

Pointing Out Other Children's Good Behavior

Russian early childhood manuals put considerable emphasis on the strategy of calling children's attention to the behavior of other children who are conducting themselves as they should. Peterina (1986) suggests sometimes inviting older children to visit younger groups to demonstrate desired behavior; young children especially like to copy older children. While it is true that the child to whom attention is being called experiences the adult's comments as praise, the target here is not this correctly behaving child, but rather the children within earshot who are not meeting expected standards.

The upbringer is actually addressing this second group of children when she enthuses, "Look how Tania is dressing herself quickly and correctly" (Kutsakova & Pushnina, 1986, p. 86). Peterina (1986) endorses this tactic because she believes it is less heavy-handed than criticism directed at offending children.   A review of my observations during lunchtime reveals many examples of this strategy.

Interestingly enough, one psychologist told me that comparing children (e.g., "Oleg cleaned up better than Sasha did") is frowned upon by Russian pedagogues. Yet, to my mind, there is only a thin line between those explicit comparisons and the only slightly more subtle comments (e.g., "Look how neatly Sasha cleaned up," said so that all can hear) that are so widely endorsed and used.

Competition

Upbringers are also encouraged to use competition to motivate children to perform as desired. Peterina (1986) suggests, for example, that upbringers wonder out loud which children will gather their dishes from the table with the least clinking. In this book, Chapter 11 contains several examples. Recall how the upbringers spurred children to eat quickly by announcing which children had finished first.

Urie Bronfenbrenner (1970b) and James Muckle (1990) have described the use of group competition in Soviet schools to motivate performance. I have seen no reference to this practice in manuals focusing on early childhood education, nor did I witness it during my observations. All competition was individual.

WHEN MISBEHAVIOR OR CONFLICTS OCCUR ANYWAY

As any teacher can tell you, one can greatly reduce the incidence of misbehavior and conflicts through wise preventative strategies, but occasional disciplinary problems are nevertheless inevitable. The teacher (or upbringer) must be prepared to deal with them. What does the early childhood literature recommend to upbringers in these situations?

Corporal punishment was not permitted in Soviet children's institutions, nor, of course, is it now. One of the items on the questionnaire I gave teachers asked them to indicate the extent of their agreement with the statement "I believe spanking to be a good child-rearing method." Out of 62 teachers who responded to the statement, only 2 (3.2%) agreed with it; 48 (77.4%) disagreed. (Interestingly enough, 12 teachers, 19.4%, were not sure.)

The fact is that I rarely saw anything one might term "punishment." Upbringers told me that they sometimes resorted to having a child sit apart from the group for a "time out" period, but I saw this happen only twice, once when two boys were fighting over blocks and once when a boy was disrupting a music lesson. In the first case, the child got up without permission after a minute or so and the upbringer seemed not to notice. In the second case, the child was ordered to sit behind the other children, but he was allowed to participate in the lesson from that vantage point. I did not find time-out discussed or recommended in early childhood manuals.

Instead, these books uniformly urge upbringers to remain calm and to find nonpunitive strategies for dealing with forgetful or angry children. Upbringers are reminded that preschool-aged children are given to imitation and that if they hear adults raise their voices or speak sharply, soon enough they too will adopt negative styles of interacting with others. The manuals further point out that harshness agitates and alienates children, making them unable or unwilling to comply with adult requests (e.g., Bogina & Terekhova, 1987; Kutsakova & Pushnina, 1986).

What then are upbringers to do? The following sections describe frequently recommended and practiced strategies.

Redirection

Upbringers learn that, particularly with very young children, redirection is an effective technique for quelling problem behavior. Bondarenko and Voronova (1986) recommend that, when two 2- or 3-year-olds are fighting over a toy, the attention of one should be diverted to another toy. Similarly, when children fight over a role, as when two children both want to be the doctor, the upbringer may suggest related roles, so that all will be satisfied. In an example proposed by Bondarenko and Voronova, one would-be doctor became a dentist, the other a veterinarian. (Recall a similar example in Chapter 7.)

Redirection is in fact a technique I saw practiced a great deal. Often, when two children argued over a toy, the upbringer would allow the child who had it first to keep it, but she would remind the loser of another toy just like it or very similar to it. For example, one day I watched as one boy tried to push another off a riding toy he wanted. The upbringer interrupted the altercation: "Sasha, why are you doing that? This isn't our only car. Take this car. It is just like that one." Another day two boys started stomping their feet and laughing while the upbringer tried to read a story to the group. The nanny told them to stop, but to no avail. The upbringer then calmly asked the nanny to escort the two boys to a table and give them something else to do. They were allowed to play with peg boards while the rest of the children listening to the rest of the story.

Using Positive Language And Explaining Reasons

Peterina (1986) writes about the importance of using conflict situations as opportunities to tell children how they should behave and why: "In [conflict situations] it is good to show children how they should act and, as best as is possible, explain why this is so. . . . A kindly tone during the discussion creates in the child a positive emotional frame of mind. Through such experiences ethical ideas are formed and strengthened within a positive environment of cultured behavior" (p. 38).

Peterina adds that adult intervention has the greatest impact when it occurs immediately after the incident in question. The upbringer should not wait. The following anecdote illustrates her point: A boy, Urie, has finished undressing after outside time and wishes to get to the playroom. A girl, Olia, is in his way–she sat down near the door to untie her shoes. Urie tries to shove her aside. The pedagogue, notes Peterina, should approach Urie and calmly coach him: "Urie, if you want to get by, you should say, 'Olia, let me pass, please.' Then Olia will get up and you will get through" (p. 38). Instead of focusing on the negative, on what Urie should *not* have done, the upbringer has framed her response as a suggestion for what he *should* do. American educators call this using "positive" language (Hildebrand, 1986).

Note, however, that Urie was not given a reason. Perhaps the reason (not hurting Olia) was thought to be so obvious that it did not need to be stated. Sometimes, however, reasons are not so obvious and need to be made explicit. American research has shown that explaining reasons to children is extremely important; children are more likely to comply with adult expectations if they understand the reasons behind them (Baumrind, 1967).

Russian early childhood manuals also support the importance of explaining to children the rationales for various rules. Upbringers are told to tell children that the reason they should put their spoons on their plates after they have eaten is so that the tables stay clean (Peterina, 1986), that the reason they should put their indoor shoes in their closets is so that they will not have to look for them after outside time, and that the reason they should hang their dresses and shirts on their chairs neatly is so that later their clothing will not be wrinkled when they put it on again (Kutsakova & Pushnina, 1986).

A number of times I overheard upbringers use reasoning to try to instill empathy. The explanations they gave often focused on the feelings of the victim after an act of aggression. One day a boy kicked over a block structure that another child had constructed. "Andriusha, you shouldn't do this at all. He let you play with him, and you destroyed his house. Why are you laughing? He built this. He tried hard. And you knocked it over." On another occasion in another center a similar incident occurred. The upbringer took the perpetrator aside. "Look what you did. Was it better before you did this or now? Yes, it was better before."

Examples of some of the other reasons for prohibitions that I overheard included not bending hula hoops because it had been very difficult to buy them and it might be impossible to replace them, not kneeling in the sand because otherwise pants will be dirtied, not dragging coats on the ground so that mothers will not have extra wash to do, not making knocking sounds because they distract other children (during a lesson), not pushing a riding toy too fast because the child on it might bump her forehead, not building block towers too tall so that they won't crash, and letting another child continue to play with a toy a little longer because he had it first.

Gerbova, Zimonina, and Pushnina (1986) suggest that it is not only the wrongdoer who should hear messages about what s/he should do and why. "Victims" in conflict situations need to learn how to use language to defend their rights. Teaching them how to talk to other children in these situations can help them learn how to be assertive without being impolite or aggressive. Gerbova and her coauthors suggest that upbringers tell children some of the words they can use in these situations. Two examples focus on children who complain that another child is claiming the toy(s) they are using: "Negotiate with Alesha yourself. Explain to him that you also need the big blocks." Or, "Sasha also wants to play with the red car. Tell him, 'I'll play with it and then give it to you. I won't forget'" (pp. 166-167).

While observing, I heard a comment along these lines only once. "Tell Lena to stop," a girl complained. "Come to an agreement yourselves," replied the upbringer. It seemed to me that the upbringer's intent was simply to brush off the problem; I did not see her comment as helpful since she did not help the girl learn *how* to "come to an agreement." Of course, it is possible that she thought that she had already taught the appropriate strategies and that now it was time for them to show that they could use them independently, without adult coaching.

Using Play Form

The reader is acquainted with the role of play form in preventing misbehavior. Play form also has an important role in situations of conflict or disobedience, when it may be used in the service of distraction or redirection. For example, one day I watched a boy who was playing house. After a while he became rowdy, apparently losing interest in what he was doing. The upbringer came over and asked him to pour her some tea. After he pretended to do so, she asked, "And what can I have to eat with my tea?" He was kept busy for a few more minutes.

Upbringers may pretend that it is not so much they as the toy animals or dolls who are dissatisfied with children's behavior. Kutsakova and Pushnina (1986) suggest that an upbringer might make a comment to the effect that "our teddy bear Toptishka has noticed that Sasha did a poor job of putting away the toys" (p. 85). In another example, a toy rabbit complains, "I don't like the way Sasha, Olia, and Vova [set the tables] today–they worked slowly, took away each other's spoons, made the tables look bad. I won't sit at their tables; I'll sit by the tables set by Sveta and Tania" (p. 89). A toy's opinion may also be used in a threatening manner: "Today Burratino [a Pinocchio-like doll] will check to see how you wash your hands–he'll see whose towel is dirty, who did a poor job soaping up his hands or rinsing them, who has moist sleeves, who did a poor job rolling them up" (p. 92).

Recall the example of a lesson on spatial concepts in Chapter 9. In that scene the upbringer pretended that Katia, a doll, wanted a child to return to the common pool the objects he had taken for himself. Sometimes it seemed as if toys were used almost as substitutes for assistant teachers.

How do educators reconcile their belief in the use of tactful positive language with the negative words dolls and toy animals are allowed to make? According to Kutsakova and Pushnina (1986), play form allows the upbringer to evaluate children's behavior objectively without hurting their feelings. It is thus assumed (erroneously, I think), that children do not realize that it is actually the adult, not the toy, who is speaking.

One day I was observing during an afternoon free play time when there were shouts from the housekeeping area. A girl was upset because she had been waiting too long to play with the toy telephone. The boy who was using it would not give it up. The upbringer approached. "What is the matter?" she asked. "There is no answer? Let's call again." The boy dialed and made ringing noises. The upbringer pretended to be the person whom he was calling and had a short conversation with him. Then she ended the conversation and handed the phone to the girl who had been waiting. To the boy, she said, "There. You got through. Now Nadia can make her call." The problem was solved, both children seemed content with the resolution.

Since this was the first time I had seen play form used to resolve a conflict, I later asked the upbringer to explain to me what she had done. "It is important to approach situations from the child's perspective, through play," she said simply. I thought for a long time about her words and the scene I had witnessed. The upbringer's caring demeanor and the apparent ease and rapidity with which she had handled a potentially explosive situation were very impressive. Perhaps, I thought, American preschool teachers should do more of this. Only a few days later did I begin to realize why they might not want to. Once again it was the adult, not the children, who was perfecting problem-solving skills. Yes, the conflict had been handled very smoothly and to everyone's satisfaction. The only trouble was that the children had not learned how to resolve their conflicts; it had been done for them.

Paying Little or No Attention to Children's Conflicts

Explaining to upbringers how they should handle children's circle-time arguments (who has to hold hands with whom, who gets to stand next to the upbringer, etc.), Boguslavskaia and Smirnova (1991) suggest a quick reminder about the rules (e.g., you have to hold hands with whoever happens to be next to you) and then dropping the subject. "It's not good to get waylaid by these conflicts; it's better to quickly and tactfully resolve [them]" (p. 21).

Indeed, I found quick responses to children's conflicts and misbehavior to be the norm in the centers in which I observed. For example, one day two children were fighting over a pillow. "Sasha and Pavlusha, figure this out amicably," the upbringer told them as she passed by. "Alesha, don't break it. You shouldn't," was all another boy heard after he knocked down another child's block structure. One boy kept bumping his car into another's. It was clearly intentional. "Play calmly. Why like this?" the upbringer asked, then patted him and walked away. "Sasha, you shouldn't hit him. Play together. Why aren't you sharing?" The question was rhetorical since the upbringer paid no further attention to the altercation. A number of times I heard upbringers respond to children's complaints about other children with such questions as, "Was it an accident?" The answer was usually in the affirmative and the matter was dropped. Occasionally, upbringers' quick comments relayed messages about chivalry. A boy and a girl were fighting over a helicopter. "Misha, give in; after all she's a girl."

Fairly often, children's squabbles were simply ignored. The American early childhood literature suggests to teachers that they sometimes ignore inappropriate behavior and conflicts so that children are not rewarded for misbehavior and have the opportunity to solve their problems themselves (e.g., Gartrell, 1987; Miller, 1984). I have not seen this practice recommended in the Russian literature, however. On the contrary, the Russian literature is consistent in endorsing high involvement by upbringers in every detail of children's upbringing. In the centers in which I observed in Moscow, perfunctory responses and lack of attention to misbehavior and conflicts were more likely the result of the limitations put upon upbringers by the low ratio of adults to children. Supporting my interpretation is the fact that when I showed Russian upbringers my slides of American teachers helping young children negotiate their disagreements, the Russian upbringers said that they were impressed and envious that the American teachers could take the time to do this.

In 1970 Bronfenbrenner (1970b) shared his impression that a principal means of discipline in Russian homes was the withdrawal of adult attention in response to misbehavior. He explained that "love withdrawal" powerfully curbs misbehavior, particularly within an otherwise loving relationship, because the child finds it painful to lose the love and warmth to which s/he is accustomed. An unfortunate by-product for the child, however, is emotional insecurity. I did not see this kind of intentional withdrawal of attention in child care centers. Two Russian psychologists whom I questioned also had not seen it there (both had had extensive experience in centers), and the practice is not recommended in the literature.

When conflicts were ignored or handled with just a quick comment by the upbringer, did the children work their problems out anyway? Frequently they did. In fact, I was surprised to see how often upbringer's quick directives were followed and how often conflicts that received no adult attention were resolved by the children themselves.

Criticizing and Shaming

It may seem strange to see a section on shaming in a chapter on discipline, and I debated with myself whether or not to write about it in this book. However, responses to my questionnaire, a look at some of the model statements presented in early childhood books, and my own observation notes convinced me that some discussion of this technique is in order. Only 26 of 62 (42%) of the upbringers who responded to my questionnaire disagreed with the item "I believe that scolding and criticism make the children I work with improve." Another 23 (37%) were unsure; 13 (21%) agreed.

A published example of scolding and criticism comes from Kutsakova's and Pushnina's (1986) chapter. They write that the upbringer should openly criticize children who do not put any effort into their work. Words on the order of "You worked poorly; you didn't try, you let yourself be distracted" (p. 95) are suggested.

My mealtime observations (described in the previous chapter) contain several examples of shaming, as when upbringers called children who were eating slowly "lazy" or wondered aloud how such a "big and strong" child could eat so poorly. Similarly, I overheard an upbringer ask a boy who would not share if he were selfish, another ask a girl "Who do you think you are, a fashion plate?"[1] when she would not buckle her shoes herself, and a nanny tell a boy that he was big enough to know better than to stack blocks higher than himself.

The most strained scene was a music lesson led by a music upbringer who later told me that she knew she was too nervous; she blamed her state of mind on her personal worries about her family during this time of economic crisis. When children did not learn dance steps as quickly as she would have liked, she accused them of "fooling around," "bothering her," "sleeping," and "not listening." At the end of the lesson, she told the children that they had upset her with their poor performance. "It's very difficult when you don't try." But then, realizing that she herself was partly responsible for the tense atmosphere in the room, she relented, "But you were trying. It just seemed to me that you were not."

Occasionally upbringers and nannies criticized children while chatting with other adults within earshot of the children themselves. Upbringers told me that one boy was a difficult child and that another drew poorly; a nanny told me which children she liked best. In both cases we were in the playroom where children could easily overhear the conversations. It seemed that children's ability to understand and take to heart adults' talk with each other was greatly underestimated.

One day during an indoor play time a boy wet his pants. The upbringer did not criticize him in any way; she just helped him change into dry clothes. Some other children gathered around and asked if he were "little." The upbringer defended him, saying that he was not, that sometimes things like this just happened. I wondered if the children's question was a consequence of having heard other upbringers call children "little" for similar incidents.

SOME CONCLUDING THOUGHTS

Of the "direct" strategies described in this chapter, three seemed to me to predominate: praise, redirection (often in play form language), and ignoring. What are the common threads among them? All contributed to the pleasant atmosphere in most of the child care groups I visited. Though some Americans would be concerned that the use of praise instead of encouragement fostered dependency, my guess is that praise did more to bolster self-confidence than to hurt it. Redirection played a key role in maintaining a peaceful climate in most groups; misbehavior and conflicts were handled smoothly (often cleverly) and did not escalate into big deals. Even ignoring might be looked at in this way.

Across strategies, another common thread was the fact that, whenever the upbringer intervened in a problem situation, it was she, not the children, who did the thinking. I never heard an upbringer ask children to think about or evaluate possible solutions to their problems. There are two indicators that this was not peculiar to the centers in which I observed. First, these centers were considered better than average. Second, despite fairly extensive reading of the Russian early childhood literature, I have nowhere come across information on guiding children through social problem-solving sequences.

Yet the recent literature presents many voices calling for more freedom for children, more "yeses than no's," more willingness by adults to be persuaded by children's ideas and opinions (e.g., Zverev, 1990). The directors and upbringers I talked to wanted this to happen, and were making moves in that direction. It was significant, for example, that children were no longer required to participate in all activities. It was also impressive that the upbringers who filled out my questionnaire rated the fostering of inquisitiveness as more important than the training of good manners and obedience (Ispa, in press). A music upbringer told me that, as a rule, younger upbringers are less strict than older ones, and children are less inhibited in younger upbringers' groups. To be sure, I saw exceptions to this generalization, but it made sense to me, given the trend toward more freedom in the society at large.

What will the future bring? To be sure recent signs point to more room for children to have a voice in decision making. Changes will take time, however. Attitudes do not change overnight. It is telling that, when asked to indicate their level of agreement with "traditional" child-rearing ideas (absolute authority of adults, superiority of rote learning, etc.), upbringers' average scores fell at "not sure," suggesting uncertainty during a time of transition (Ispa, in press).

Besides educational professionals and the press, an additional source of influence will surely be parents. Both in the 1970s and in 1991 I heard parents complain about regimentation in child care centers. This message comes through in the popular press also (e.g., Shilova, 1993). Parents want more attention to their children as individuals, and many want them to experience more freedom. With the privatization of child care centers in a market economy, the need to attract paying customers (parents) may well be an important stimulus for change.

NOTE

1. A translation that might better transmit the flavor of this comment would be, "Who do you think you are, a *princess*?" During the years of communist rule, people who were concerned with clothing fashion were considered bourgeois, uppity, and lazy.

Chapter 13

Relationships with Parents

"Parents are the child's first upbringers; because of this their role in personality development is enormous" (Ostrovskaiia, 1990, p. 5). Soviet, and now Russian, educators recognize that children are tremendously influenced by conditions within their families. They also recognize that their own ability to influence children hinges on children's experiences at home. "The effectiveness of pedagogical influence depends greatly on the family microclimate; the child is more receptive to our upbringing efforts if he grows in an atmosphere of friendship, trust, and mutual affection" (Ostrovskaiia, 1990, p. 5).

PARENT-UPBRINGER CONTINUITY AND MUTUAL REGARD

Educators believe that, for the optimal development of children, there should be continuity between the home and center in child-rearing expectations and practices. The two settings should supplement, not conflict with, one another. Communication and mutual understanding between parents and upbringers is therefore regarded as of crucial importance (Ostrovskaiia, 1987, 1990; Peterina, 1986).

Does continuity actually exist? Questionnaire data that I collected from mothers and upbringers about their child-rearing ideas and feelings would suggest that it does (Ispa, in press). Upbringers and high-school-educated mothers gave similar answers on all eight child-rearing constructs measured by my questionnaire. Upbringers and college-educated mothers differed only in terms of the importance they accorded rule conformity–the mothers thought it less important. Mothers with technical institute training differed from upbringers only in that mothers were more likely to feel powerless vis a vis their children (found it harder to say no). Though both of these differences were statistically significant, they were of very low magnitude–less than one point on the 10-point Rule-Conformity scale and less than half a point on the 5-point Powerlessness scale.

Moreover, there were no differences between mothers and upbringers on six scales assessing opinions about the importance of inquisitiveness or peer orientation, agreement with authoritarian child-rearing ideas and collectivist values (putting the group's needs above the individual's), in beliefs that they should be involved in every detail of children's lives, or in feelings of closeness to and enjoyment of children.

Unfortunately, the questionnaire did not include questions measuring the attitudes of parents and upbringers toward each other. Despite the fact that upbringers and parents seemed to hold similar ideas about child-rearing, my impression was that in many cases mutual suspicion and lack of respect color their relationship.

In Chapter 12 I mentioned that parents routinely voice concern that their children receive too little individual attention and warmth and are too regimented in child care centers. Parents also worry that their children fall ill more frequently in child care than they would if they were kept at home. These issues are behind the large numbers of mothers who take advantage of maternal-leave stipends to stay home while their children are of preschool age (see Chapter 2).

On the other side of the fence, upbringers and directors talk of serious deficiencies in parents. When I asked directors and upbringers to tell me what was hardest about their jobs, the answer was often "parents." Three of the six directors and one pediatrician whom I interviewed maintained that parents are not as child centered as they should be or as parents were in the 1960s and 1970s. They saw parental inattentiveness as responsible for discipline problems and children's slowed language development.

A middle-aged upbringer complained that "parents don't talk to their children enough. While they are walking home or to the center they could talk about the seasons, or point out how the trees are changing. They just walk in silence." The director of her center defended the parents, interjecting that these days parents have no time, that they are worn out from having to stand in line after work to buy bare necessities. "No," responded the upbringer, not accepting this excuse. "They have to walk with their children anyway to bring them to the center; they may as well talk, explain things. Then the children wouldn't draw such strange trees because they would have noticed what trees are really like." Later I was to see a nearly identical lament in a newspaper article urging parents of preschoolers to do a better job of preparing them for school ("Dlia vas," 1993).

Along the same lines, directors and upbringers criticized parents for not heeding their advice, not listening to the child-rearing information they are given. When I told a director that I appreciated the training in politeness at her center, she accepted the compliment but grumbled that parents do not follow through, thereby limiting the effectiveness of upbringers' efforts. Later she talked about a child who seemed to have no respect for others. She blamed the problem on parents who spoil him, give him everything he wants. "He brags that he has everything under his couch at home. The upbringer tries to bring him down. She comments on other children's nice clothing and then asks him, `Do *you* have such a coat under your couch?'"

In addition to dissatisfaction with parents' child-rearing skills, there were bad feelings about their aloofness toward center staff members. One woman who had directed a center for 20 years told me that parents are not as friendly and respectful as they used to be. "At pick-up time they just grab their children and run. They don't stick around anymore to chat." Another director similarly said that she used to feel closer to parents.

I heard that, furthermore, in the past parents showed more gratitude. In fact, some parents whose children had attended the center many years ago still offered more help than parents of currently enrolled children. To illustrate, one director told about a father whose child had graduated from her center years ago. He was employed as a truck driver. The other day he had called her to ask if her center needed frying pans; he was delivering some to stores. Indeed her kitchen did need a new frying pan, and the next day he brought one. (I wondered, but did not ask, if he was actually stealing state property for the benefit of the center.)

A music upbringer had her own story. A few days before we talked, she had been waiting at a bus stop when a mother and child arrived. She knew them from the center where she worked. No conversation ensued; the mother never even said hello. The upbringer was upset by this episode because she saw it as symptomatic of the alienation many parents feel from child care institutions. A director who was listening to this story nodded. "Yes," she said, "today's parents might say hello if they see you in the child care center but ignore you if by chance they see you elsewhere." Only one director disagreed with this picture. She had directed a center for 30 years and had noticed no change in parents' friendliness over that time.

A pediatrician and a psychologist with whom I spoke also commented that parents are more hassled and less attentive than parents were a decade or two ago. They thought the current economic situation was just one of the factors involved. For one, they said, many parents of the 1990s are coping with divorce. Moreover, grandparents are not as available as they were for the previous generation; either they are at work themselves, or they have less interest than their own parents did in pitching in to care for grandchildren. The burden of parenting is made even more difficult by current cynicism about government and the absence of clear moral convictions. Learning about the abuses of Joseph Stalin and other former heroes, and hearing previous moral values (such as atheism and socialism) derided, adults do not know in whom or in what to believe. The results, they explained, have been widespread apathy and disrespect for authority, plus a growing feeling that honest work will not get one far. How can parents communicate clear standards to children when they themselves are unsure about what is right and what is wrong?

There is evidence that American early childhood teachers similarly hold negative perceptions of parents (Kontos, Raikes, & Woods, 1983). However, it seems to me that there is an important difference between the two countries, and that is in the tone of articles and books for teachers about working with parents. My impression is that the Russian sources convey more negative messages about parents; they are more likely to indicate that parents "commonly" have certain failings, particularly in the moral upbringing they provide. While American teachers may hold similar opinions, it seems to me that the literature they read holds out a more sympathetic view of parents. The American literature is certainly more likely to urge teachers to expect to learn from, as well as to teach, parents.

AVENUES FOR UPBRINGER-PARENT COMMUNICATION

How and when do upbringers and parents communicate? The remainder of the chapter describes informal and structured opportunities for parent education and involvement.

Home Visits

Upbringers are told that they can work more effectively with children and give better advice to parents if they know something about conditions in each child's home. Directors told me that almost all families are visited at home at least once, either just before or soon after their children first begin attending their programs. Though Peterina (1986) writes about the advisability of two home visits per year, my understanding was that in most cases the introductory visit is both the first and the last one. (This was corroborated in a telephone conversation with a director in December, 1993.) One director told me that the probability of a second home visit is greater for families who live nearby or whose children seem troubled.

The purpose of home visits, according to both directors and published sources (e.g., Peterina, 1986), is to gain a better understanding of the child and to give concrete advice to parents. Upbringers try to make the visits seem informal and relaxed so that they may establish a personal relationship with members of the family.

Seminars for Parents

Educational parent meetings, or seminars, are held about four times a year. They may be led by center staff or by invited speakers, such as pediatricians. Popular topics include the daily routine and curricula at the center, safeguarding children's health, the importance of play and how to play with children, appropriate expectations for children's behavior, and discipline (Ostrovskaiia, 1990; Peterina, 1986).

Though discussion during these meetings is encouraged, control is actually in the hands of the seminar leader. "The upbringer summarizes [parents'] statements, calls attention to the more successful ones, and shows them the correct way to solve problems" (Ostrovskaiia, 1990, p. 4). Thus discussions are viewed as opportunities for teaching by center staff, not as opportunities for real give-and-take and mutual education among parents and upbringers.

Written Materials

As parents walk through the center each day, they typically pass by a number of large posters in the central foyer just inside the main door, in the hallways, and in the dressing rooms. Common themes for these posters include reminders about the importance of following a daily routine at home consistent with the one followed in the center, suggestions about physical exercises appropriate for home, and warnings about common home safety hazards. Often there are also examples of children's art work. The placement of these works–at adult eye-level–makes it clear that they are on display for parents' and visitors' enjoyment more than for children's. (Recall that children's art was not displayed in playrooms or in music/gym rooms.)

Also in the central foyer and/or in the dressing rooms there may be shelves of books, flyers, and magazines on various child-rearing topics. Parents may check these out to read at home.

Informal Parent-Upbringer Contacts

As indicated in Chapter 5, informal contacts between parents and upbringers are limited by the policy of not allowing parents into the playroom. The only exceptions are for parents of new children who are still adjusting, "open house" days when parents may visit during the day, and during holiday celebrations. Parents are asked to change into indoor shoes for these occasions.

When I commented to an upbringer that in the American centers with which I am familiar, parents come right into the classroom to pick up their children, she was shocked. "But we let our children crawl on the floor," she protested, implying that adequate cleanliness could not be maintained if parents came in in their soiled outdoor shoes and boots. One late afternoon I saw her look up to see a mother at the doorway. "Vasia has been coughing a little today," she notified the mother. The mother looked worried but only nodded. Later that week I saw this upbringer go into the dressing room for a few minutes to talk to a mother who had come to pick up her child. While they talked, the children in the playroom were unsupervised.

The policy of not allowing parents into the playroom seems to make it harder than it otherwise would be to get children to leave at departure time. Many times I watched as parents leaned into the playroom from the dressing room doorway, urging their reluctant children to put toys away so that they could leave for home. The upbringers did not help, and some parents seemed to feel helpless. I remember one father who kept reminding his son that he had little cars at home too, and an exasperated mother who finally pretended to leave, scaring her daughter into following her. Surely it would be easier for these parents if they could have entered the playroom to affectionately greet their children and help them put their toys away. A director disagreed with me; she thought rather that children want to stay longer at the center because "parents nowadays are so tense and worried about everything. Upbringers maintain professional calm. The children like that."

Parents who come during the afternoon outside time need not go inside to pick up their children. This makes parent-child reunions easier, but it does not seem to result in increased upbringer-parent contact. Whether indoors or out, most parents simply said hello to the upbringer and then waited for their children to get ready to leave. [I might add that, unfortunately, minimal parent-teacher communication is the typical pattern in the United States, as well (Hogan, Ispa, & Thornburg, 1992; Powell, 1989)].

When Upbringers or Parents Bring up a Problem

Remembering having read about former practices such as embarrassing parents of difficult children by informing their supervisors at work of the problem, I asked if calls are made to parents' work places when their children are hard to handle. "Never!" exclaimed one director. Either a home visit would be scheduled, or the parents and upbringers would meet at the center to discuss the child's behavior. In these situations parents are often given information about child-rearing practices they should be using at home.

I also asked if parents ever give directors or upbringers advice, or ever indicate disagreement with the child care practices in the center. The question was greeted with laughter and another exclamation of "never!" It seemed that center staff do not ask for or receive suggestions from parents; in fact, the very idea seemed ludicrous to them. One director did, however, bring up a case she had dealt with not long ago. Parents had come to her to complain about an upbringer she had just hired. This upbringer, according to the director, was big and gruff, and the children were unhappy in her care. In fact, they cried in the mornings and resisted coming to the center. The parents wanted the director to fire the upbringer.

Firing someone, however, was a complicated matter under Soviet policies (see Chapter 3). The director spoke with the upbringer several times, but nothing seemed to change. Finally she scheduled an evening meeting between the upbringer and the parents. The upbringer explained herself, apparently to the parents' satisfaction, for after this things settled down. I asked the director if the parents had ever ventured to speak directly with the upbringer before the meeting. "No, they would be afraid that she might get angry and take it out on their children," the director explained. "Parents might ask an upbringer to help their child so he won't be unhappy, but they wouldn't confront her about her style. They would tell me instead."

Parent Committees

Parent committees are composed of at least one representative from each children's group. These individuals help the center in a number of ways. Some parents may have connections with supply sources through their own work or through personal friendships. These parents are in a position to advocate the center's needs for sufficient and timely deliveries. Members of the parent committee may help directors and upbringers make informational posters for parents. They may organize other parents to help with building repair, yard work, sewing (of curtains or children's costumes, for example), or construction of handmade toys. Qualified parents may be asked to participate in inspections; it is understood that parents are being educated (about hygiene, nutrition, etc.) even as they check on center operations. Finally, parent committee members may be called upon to work with individual families considered to need extra attention and counseling (Alekseeva, Druzhinina, & Ladodo, 1990; Peterina, 1986).

Saturday Work Days

Once or twice a year parents are asked to join the center staff on a Saturday morning to assist with a variety of tasks such as toy repair, toy construction, and yard work. In April, for example, parents of children in one center were asked to help clear the play yard of debris and to plant flowers and bushes. At another center, fathers (not mothers!) were invited to come on a Saturday in October to help plant some new bushes and fir trees and to replace a fence.   Parents are asked but not pressured to participate; upbringers have no choice.   I once wondered aloud whether upbringers resented this requirement, but it seemed that it was accepted as part of the job.   The parent committee helps to solicit help and organize chores for these Saturdays.

One director told me that she tries to keep the number of Saturday work days to a minimum because she knows parents are very busy.   On the other hand, she frequently asks individual parents for help with specific tasks.   The tasks are usually things parents can do at home, such as typing or sewing children's costumes for an upcoming holiday celebration.   Sometimes she asks for copies from parents who have access to photocopy machines at their places of work.   Before the New Year, she asks parents to provide presents that can be given to the children during the holiday celebration at the center.

CHANGES IN THE OFFING

The founders of Soviet early childhood education imagined that children would benefit in two ways–directly through their own experiences in preschool and indirectly through the education parents would get in correct child-rearing values and techniques (see Chapter 2).   For many years, parent education was guided by the notion that educators should be the givers and parents the receivers of expert advice on child rearing.   Professionals would teach and parents would listen.   Recently there has been a move away from that model toward one that advocates mutual respect and joint decision making between educators and parents (Grebennikov & Kovin'ko, 1990).

Lena Nikitina (1990) writes admiringly about an experimental center where rules have been relaxed to allow parents to visit their children in the playrooms whenever they wish, where parents are not made to feel bad if they bring their children late or pick them up early (see Chapter 6 for the more typical situation), and where, most importantly, upbringers welcome parents as equal partners in the work of child rearing.   In Nikitina's book, the chapter describing this center is optimistically entitled "My Trip into the Future."

Chapter 14

What We Think of Each Other's Programs

Before leaving for Moscow, I took slides in two high-quality non-profit child care centers in Columbia, Missouri. Using these slides, I developed a presentation showing typical events and activities in these centers. The presentation follows the daily routine in chronological order; it opens with pictures of children arriving with their parents in the morning and ends with them preparing to leave in the evening.

I showed these slides at the centers I visited in Moscow. Sometimes directors asked for a second showing, and staff from neighboring centers were invited. The presentations were always during nap times; nannies stayed with the children so that upbringers could attend.

I also took slides in the centers I visited in Moscow. I have arranged these slides to show each segment of the daily routine in the Russian centers. During the past two years I have shown them to many American early childhood teachers, administrators, and students.

In both countries educators have shown great interest in learning about early childhood practices in the other culture. I too have learned some things during the presentations. The comments and questions posed by my audiences have provided me with valuable insights into similarities and differences between the two cultures in beliefs about center-based child care. In Russia I was sometimes heard puzzlement, even laughter, about American practices I had previously taken for granted. Listening to my American viewers, I have usually heard echoes of my own feelings or thoughts, but occasionally even here I have been surprised. In this chapter I share the reactions of Russian educators to American practices, and the reactions of American educators to Russian practices.

To appreciate the reactions of my Russian viewers, the reader first needs to know a little about the centers on which I based my presentation about American child care practices.

THE AMERICAN CENTERS

One of the centers in which I took slides is the Hinkson Children's Center in Columbia; many of the children in this center are from low-income families. The second was the Child Development Laboratory of the University of Missouri Department of Human Development and Family Studies. Most of the children in this center are from middle- and upper-middle-class families. The curricula of the two centers are similar in a number of ways. Both encourage initiation by children as well as by adults, opportunities for children to be active learners, and the fostering of curiosity, creativity, and positive social skills. In both, teachers use an authoritative disciplinary style and try to meet children's individual needs as well as the needs of the group as a whole.

Though the classrooms in both centers are arranged in age-appropriate interest areas, the equipment and furnishings are rather modest. As in many American centers, the teachers often must make do with "found materials," and it is clear that aesthetic considerations have been secondary. Neither center has separate dressing rooms or bedrooms; instead children put their belongings in cubbies near the classroom doorways and, at nap time, sleep on cots scattered about the classrooms.

The teacher-child ratio at the Hinkson Children's Center is 2:18 for classrooms with 3- to 6-year-olds and 2:13 for classrooms of 2-year-olds. The ratio of staff teachers to children is 2:20 for classrooms with 2 1/2- to 5-year-olds at the Child Development Laboratory, but the inclusion of student teachers lowers the actual ratio to about 5:20. Most of the teachers at the Hinkson Children's Center have bachelor's degrees in early childhood education or a related field. At the Child Development Laboratories, the head teachers have master's degrees, and the assistant teachers have bachelor's degrees in either child development or early childhood education. *Child* magazine has named the Child Development Laboratory one of the ten best child care centers in America (Black, 1992).

I should add that I always began my talks to Russian educators by telling them that no single educational philosophy is followed in all American preschools, and that, sadly, many American preschools leave much to be desired. I explained that I thought the centers I was about to show them were representative of American preschools that provide very good or excellent care based on the educational principles endorsed by the National Association for the Education of Young Children (Bredekamp, 1987). I thought I was presenting them with a fair comparison, since the Moscow centers were also judged to be of high quality based on their own national criteria.

REACTIONS OF RUSSIAN EDUCATORS TO AMERICAN PRACTICES

"Children are children," a Russian director commented. She was struck by similarities in the scheduling of breakfast, lunch, nap, and snack times in the two countries and by the fact that American children, like Russian children, enjoy active play during indoor and outdoor free play times. My Russian hosts were somehow comforted especially by the fact that nap time is at about the same time and lasts about the same amount of time in both countries.

As might be expected, however, most of the remarks I heard reflected perceptions of Russian-American differences. Even though there may have been more similarities than differences, it was probably more interesting to talk about the latter. Most comments had to do with practices related to room decor and equipment, health and cleanliness, freedom and control, discipline and the amount of individual attention given children, and teachers' work loads and pay. Below I treat each of these issues in turn.

Russian Responses to American Room Decor and Equipment

In my experience, people in the former Soviet Union tend to have an exaggerated view of American wealth. It was therefore with some surprise that my Russian audiences learned that each American child care group usually has only one classroom and a bathroom to itself, that a separate dressing room or bedroom is unlikely. They were also surprised to see how simply, even drably, some of these rooms are furnished and decorated. Were there really no curtains, only shades? Where were the dolls' clothes? Was that all there was in the housekeeping area?

A few items drew positive comment: the brightness of plastic toys (there were complaints that their plastic toys are dull colored and break easily), having children's art hanging on the walls (none was displayed in the Russian classrooms), the sand tables, play-doh, and geoboards. (I was asked for instructions on how to make the latter two).

Russian Reactions to American Health and Cleanliness Practices

As the reader surely knows by now, Russian child care workers devote considerable energy to safeguarding children's health. My Russian audiences were startled to learn that in America children from different groups do not have separate outdoor play areas (see Chapter 5), and that we do not impose quarantines. In Russia, if a child is diagnosed with an infectious disease, his or her entire group is quarantined. This means that for the duration of the illness, until it is judged to have stopped spreading, no new children are admitted to that group, and the group is separated from others as much as possible. All dishes used by the group are kept separate, all soft toys are put away, and all other toys are washed more frequently than usual. The length of the quarantine differs depending on the specific illness.

When I told one group of directors that some American parents deliberately expose their children to chicken pox so that they will catch it while they are still little, there were looks of amazement around the table. But then one director volunteered that maybe this made sense; she thought that Russians try too hard to protect children from infections and that children therefore grow up with too few immunities. Besides, she added, she thought their efforts at guarding children from the germs of children in other groups really don't work; illnesses spread from group to group anyway. Others thought our milder climate and better food allowed us the luxury of being less vigilant about sickness.

We also talked about children staying home when they are sick. When I told them that, after a diagnosis of strep throat most American children stay home only a day or two, until the antibiotic has taken effect and they are no longer contagious, a pediatrician told me that Russian children would stay home two weeks with the same illness. As we talked, it became clear that there are two motivating factors. First, American medications are more effective than those available in Russia; a child will probably recover more quickly in America. Second, the mother of an ill child in Russia would get a leave from work with pay. This leave does not reduce her vacation time. To stay home with an ill child, the American parent may have to take leave without pay or lose vacation or personal sick days.

There was also amazement at what seemed a lackadaisical attitude among Americans about cleanliness. Do we really allow teachers and parents to come into our classrooms wearing their outdoor shoes? Is it true that children may even leave their boots on inside? One of my slides shows a girl napping in jeans with soiled knees. How could she get a good rest that way?

Not only did my Russian viewers see that American preschoolers take off only their shoes to take naps, but also that they sleep on cots scattered about the classroom. Sheets are of synthetic materials, not cotton. Some children use blankets; some do not. The sleeping arrangements depicted in my slides of American centers certainly do not look nearly as cozy as those in the Russian centers. My Russian friends acknowledged that there were some centers in Russia without separate bedrooms, but I could see that they were quite surprised at the lack of proper bedding and the absence of bedrooms even in better-than-average American centers. "Our doctors tell us that you cannot get fully rested if you don't undress and sleep in a good bed!" one director exclaimed. Others thought permanent press sheets must be terribly uncomfortable. I countered that our children seem refreshed when they awake, but she was unconvinced.

I had the feeling that our napping arrangements seemed almost uncivilized to the Russian educators. The strongest reaction came from the youngest (32-year-old) director. "I think it is better in our country," she said. "Our center is a temple where parents leave what is most precious to them." The implication was that it was not so in the two American centers she had just seen.

There was also some talk about the fact that American children and teachers seem to sit on the floor a lot, even for story listening and singing activities. Russian children may sit on the floor to build with blocks, but rarely at other times. During lessons and when upbringers read to them, children typically sit on small chairs arranged in a semicircle or in rows facing the upbringer. Why not on the floor? At first I thought it was due to concerns about floors being cold and dirty, but one director suggested that there was more to it than that. "If they sit on the floor very much, their legs will be too short," she explained.

On a related note, upbringers reacted with laughter to the fairly large number of slides showing American teachers on their knees or even sitting on the floor. Upbringers wondered how they do it; it seemed they thought it rather strenuous. "Look, she was on her knees before; now she is actually sitting on the floor!" they giggled.

As might be expected, there were also questions about mealtimes in American centers. My lunchtime slides show children serving themselves. Upbringers asked how that works, if we worry that children might take too much for themselves, not leaving enough for others.

One of my slides shows a child playing during snack time. I explained that he was not hungry, so he did not have to come to the tables. It was surprising to my Russian audience that a child would be allowed to skip snack. I detected some concern regarding their own practice of urging children to eat as much as possible. One upbringer thought (incorrectly, I think) that American children are thinner; she wondered if Russian children are overfed. Someone joked that perhaps that was why there was a food shortage in Russia. Other comments were nonevaluative and on the order of "You don't serve soup every day" or "You don't boil milk or canned vegetables" or "You serve factory-prepared foods to children! That makes it so much easier than here!"

The reader will recall, from Chapter 3, that directors and upbringers feel quite hassled by the monthly health and safety inspections their centers undergo. Yet they expressed mixed feelings about the relative freedom of American centers from such frequent checking. On the one hand, they saw the value of these inspections to ensure cleanliness and good care of children, but at the same time they were envious of American teachers and directors for not having to be on guard as much as they.

Russian Reactions to American Ideas on Freedom and Control

My Russian friends were very interested in the amount of freedom they saw given to American children. Some upbringers found it hard to understand why we do not teach young children how to draw specific shapes (see Chapters 8 and 9). One criticized American teachers for randomly choosing colors of paint to put out for children's use. (She advocated choosing colors and color combinations in such a way as to first focus children's attention on the colors of the spectrum, then on variations of these colors.)

At the same time, there were also many favorable comments about American children's opportunities to apply paint freely on large pieces of paper and to mold play-doh as they wish.

Upbringers wished their girls were also allowed to dress comfortably in pants (skirts or dresses were required at their centers). Most of all, however, they liked the fact that children's relationships with teachers seemed less top-down in the American centers. Several thought that American children must as a consequence be less nervous than Russian children.

Not only did the Russian educators notice that there are fewer regulations for children in America, but also that there are fewer for teachers. I have already shared their thoughts about external inspections. They also envied American teachers and directors for having the right to determine the daily schedules for their classrooms themselves.

Russian Reactions to American Ideas on Discipline and Individualized Attention

The slides I brought with me to Moscow show several scenes of American teachers handling disciplinary situations. Each of these scenes is several slides long. In one, a child has refused to put away some toys he has finished using. The teacher tells him he may not play with anything else until he has cleaned up; she also does not permit another child to help him. She watches the child who needs to clean up for about 10 minutes, until he has complied.

In another scene in the same classroom, a girl hits a boy because he will not share a toy. The boy ignores her and seems not to be bothered by the hit. The teacher (the same one involved in the cleanup situation) comes over and tells the boy that he should tell the girl that she may not hurt him. Next the teacher spends a long time talking to the girl, asking her to tell what happened and explaining that she must use words, not fists, when she is unhappy about something. The girl refuses to speak and starts crying. She is told to sit in a chair apart from the other children until she is ready to talk. After a few minutes, the teacher returns to the girl and, holding her affectionately, repeats the rules about talking instead of hitting. She ends by telling the girl about all the interesting activities that are planned for that day.

The reactions to these scenes were interesting. Some thought that the teacher was too severe in both cases. Why not let the other child clean up for the one who didn't want to? Isn't the second child's helpfulness to be encouraged, not discouraged? Wouldn't the first child have learned something from that, too? Maybe another time he would help the second child. Also, why insist on a reaction from the boy who was hit when he was willing to let it go? A few upbringers said they thought the American teacher did the right thing in both cases.

The one point of agreement for everyone was that the teacher should be admired for how hard she worked and how much she seemed to care about each child. "The teacher could have just sat back, but she *worked* and she showed the children a lot of attention," someone said. In general, upbringers were impressed that the American teachers spent so much time with individual children, talking to them eye-to-eye. Interestingly, one director who disagreed with the teacher's tactic in the cleanup scene commented that it took so much effort to sit with the child; it looked like it was so hard for her. This seemed to be part of her argument against the teacher's strategy.

Many times upbringers tried to reconcile what they perceived to be their own inability to provide sufficient individual attention to children, relative to what they saw American teachers doing, by pointing to the adult to child ratios in their centers. One day a pediatrician who came to see my slides noted that she was surprised that many American children under the age of 2 attend centers; Russian mothers are trying to stay home with children that young. When I told her that the ratio of teachers to children of that age is 1 to 4 in Missouri, she laughed and said that then it was all right, almost like home, in American centers.

Russian Reactions Concerning Teacher Compensation in the United States

The discussions often touched on teacher compensation. Up-bringers had not expected to learn that in America, as in their country, salaries and social status are low for preschool teachers. There was considerable comment about the fact that American teachers work longer days than they (eight as compared to six hours per day), have only two weeks of paid vacation time per year (upbringers are entitled to six), and have no guaranteed maternity leave benefits. Upbringers were surprised to hear that they thus seemed to be in the better position. On the other hand, one upbringer commented that "I'd rather work eight hours and not have to stand in line after work for two hours to buy food for my family. I feel like I work eight hours a day too. I'd rather spend those two extra hours here in the center than in line at a store."

One of the American teachers shown in my slides was seven months pregnant when I took the photographs. Seeing an obviously pregnant woman sit on the floor to lead circle time, kneel on the floor to talk to children, and handle discipline problems, resulted in general amazement. In their country, a woman at this stage of pregnancy would have been on paid maternity leave. When I explained the sorry state of "family leave" in the United States, the Russian upbringers and directors saw an advantage to their way of life. One curriculum specialist, however, mused that Americans and Russians must have a "different psychology" about pregnancy. In Russia, she said, women know that their leave is coming up, and they worry that perhaps their doctor tricked them by writing down a late due date, thereby cheating them out of some of their maternity leave. She thought that perhaps women expect to feel too uncomfortable to work when maybe actually they might be fine if they had no way out. (The law stipulates full pay from 70 days before a woman's due date to 70 days after childbirth.)

REACTIONS OF AMERICAN EDUCATORS TO RUSSIAN PRACTICES

In testimony to lingering effects of the cold war, a number of American teachers who have viewed my slides of Russian child care centers have expressed surprise that Russian upbringers seem so caring, kind, and personable. One particularly open woman even admitted to being surprised to discover that Russian children are "just as cute as American children." She went on to explain herself: "I don't know why I thought they'd be different. I guess it's because I remember hiding under my desk during air raid drills when I was in elementary school. These are the people we were taught to protect ourselves against!"

Other reactions I have regularly encountered revolve around some of the same issues brought up by my Russian audiences: room decor and equipment, maintenance of health and cleanliness, freedom versus control, discipline, and individualized attention.

American Reactions to Russian Room Decor and Equipment

When, after a presentation, I have asked my American audiences to tell me what most impressed them about Russian child care, the most frequent responses have had to do with the beds and bedrooms. Americans are amazed at how comfortable the sleeping arrangements are for Russian children. Some laugh, thinking how appalled their Russian counterparts must be at the helter-skelter arrangements in American centers. Comparing the separate bedrooms and cozy beds enjoyed in the Russian centers with the cots scattered around their own classrooms, American teachers say it must be easier to get children to sleep in the former situation. They also comment that it would be easier to clean up the classroom after lunch if the children were in another room. Yet most don't think all this matters for the quality of children's sleep.

There have also been many remarks about the tidiness of the rooms in the Russian centers and the fact that the children eat on china (not plastic) dishes. Some American teachers have exclaimed that they can't imagine their children keeping everything in its place so nicely ("Our children rearrange the housekeeping area every day!") or handling breakable dishes carefully enough. Some have said they like the Oriental-style rugs in the Russian playrooms but that "they wouldn't stay clean in our rooms." Some teachers are impressed by the fact that upbringers take the time to comb girls' hair after nap time; others, however, have wondered why children are dressed and groomed "as if for church just to go to preschool."

In general the slides have moved teachers to think about their commitments to two values: neatness and freedom. They have wondered whether it is possible to have both the orderliness and eye appeal of the Russian playrooms, and the messy activities and freedom to change things around that they believe to be so important for young children.

The one other comment American teachers make about the equipment they see in the Russian centers is that the toys seem dull colored compared to American materials for children. Russians would agree.

American Reactions to Russian Health and Cleanliness Practices

After the beds and bedrooms, what impresses American educators most about Russian child care is the amount of time upbringers and nannies devote to ensuring cleanliness and good health in children. Interestingly, they are impressed not because they think all the practices are necessary for children's well-being, but simply because they see them as evidence of the Russians' concern for children.

One day I showed some of my slides to my sixth grade son's class. When I showed them the Russian outdoor play areas, I asked them to think why it might be that children of different groups play separately. Though there were many guesses, no one came up with the right answer. (They thought it might be to cut down on fighting between groups, to lower the probability of toys getting lost, to make it easier for each teacher to keep track of all the children in her group, and so on.) That it might have something to do with safeguarding health never even occurred to these American children.

I have not engaged my adult audiences in such guessing games, but their comments make it clear that they too think that having separate but adjacent play areas is an unnecessary precaution. ("Germs will pass around anyway.") Moreover, they think that training resistance to the cold, having children walk on slats to prevent fallen arches, and using ultraviolet light to kill germs are quaint but useless practices. Some like seeing children undress for naps, but most think it of no consequence for the quality of their sleep.

Gasps often follow my statement that Russian children spend three hours outside each day even in very cold weather. One teacher reported that she had heard teachers from the northern states (e.g., Minnesota) say they would like children to spend more time outdoors in winter, but that teachers cannot rely on parents to supply sufficiently warm clothing.

My slides of meals in Russian centers also elicit many comments. The fact that lunch is a three-course affair astonishes American educators. They also are surprised that Russian children do not serve themselves and that upbringers do not sit with children at the table. Most are quite critical of the fact that Russian children are not permitted to talk during meals and that those who are slow to eat are either verbally hurried or spoonfed. They see casual mealtime conversation as important for children, and urging or forcing them to eat more than they want as possibly leading to eating problems later in life. "Children will eat if they are hungry!" they exclaim. "If they don't want to eat, they shouldn't have to."

Another issue that provokes discussion among my American viewers is toilet training. One teacher said, "I never realized 'potty training' might actually happen with *pots*!" There is consternation at the thought of having to clean the pots; the American teachers who work with toddlers have access to small toilets or child-sized toilet seat inserts.

Many are also surprised at the use of cotton towels. Several have said they realize now what a luxury (and how wasteful) it is to have throwaway paper towels.

American Reactions to Russian Ideas on Freedom and Control

As mentioned earlier, freedom of choice is an important issue during meal times. It also comes up in regard to lessons and indoor play.

My American audiences regularly express concern about the lack of opportunity for Russian children to make choices and express their creativity during lessons. One American director said that the appliqué lesson on making ducks out of precut circles (described in Chapter 9) reminded her of "bad second grade." Another director was adamant that it is wrong to require children to draw grass (or anything else).

One teacher shared with me the notes she took during one of my presentations. One section was about indoor play time. She had written, "In Russia, the teacher directs a lot of the activities and also teaches children how to play. As an example of this, when the children in Russia were playing doctor, the teacher would interject and tell them when they should give a shot. This teacher perceived her role in children's play as that of 'director.' The American teacher sees herself as more of a 'guide.'"

Another set of comments relevant to the issue of freedom concerns children's and upbringers' clothing. Two upbringers in my slides are wearing pants, but the rest are wearing dresses or skirts and blouses, and some are wearing high heels. All of the girls are in skirts or dresses and many have, in typical Russian style, big beautiful bows in their hair. Americans felt that dressing like this was too formal, too restricting. Some were also perplexed by the robes a few upbringers still wear. (Recall, from Chapter 3, Note 3, that robes are now optional for upbringers.)

American Reactions to Russian Ideas on Discipline and Individualized Attention

As noted in the opening paragraph of Chapter 12, many American educators has expressed admiration and wonder at how well behaved and polite the Russian children in my slides appear to be. A variety of responses have greeted my explanations of the disciplinary strategies used in the Russian centers.

The reaction of Americans that has surprised me most is in connection with the Russian practice of pretending that dolls and stuffed toy animals are giving directions and evaluations. Many

Americans have laughed when I have explained how this is done; questioning them, I have discovered that it was often nervous laughter I was hearing. Discomfort with the practice stems from Americans' likening of the doll to "big brother," or to a "bad guy" who does the teacher's "dirty work" (telling children what to do and what they have done wrong). Though I have stressed that the toys also bring interesting activities to the children and compliment them on good performance, the general reaction of my viewers has remained negative.

American teachers do like the Russian upbringers' "minimizing" of disciplinary situations, and they have been impressed with upbringers' use of play form to redirect children (except when play form involves talking through dolls). They appreciate that children are usually not made to feel that they are bad children. Some, though, have pointed out that the children are not being taught how to solve interpersonal problems, that only the upbringers are being creative problem solvers.

Many American teachers are shocked that Russian teachers must work with adult:child ratios of 1:20. They exclaim that they find their own 2:20 ratios challenging. Some have commented that their respect for the Russian upbringers is doubled when they see that the Russians try to do so much for children with so little help.

A LAST WORD

In this chapter I have shared the negative, the positive, and the puzzled comments of the Russian and American educators who have viewed my slides of one another's programs. I would like to end this chapter by emphasizing that, despite some questions and some criticisms, educators in both countries came away from the presentations with words of respect for one another.

The final slide in my presentation about American child care shows two teachers smiling at the camera. One of my more touching memories is of Russian directors and upbringers waving at this slide, telling me to give their regards and best wishes to the American teachers. "They are our partners; we have the same goals–the happiness and well-being of children." Similar sentiments were sent back to them from this side of the world.

Chapter 15

What Next?

Much has happened since I left Moscow in 1991. The Soviet Union is no more. Much communist dogma has been rejected. Religious belief has become acceptable, even popular. A fledgling market economy has brought with it privatization of factories, stores, and services. It has also brought runaway inflation. What has all of this meant for child care?

To find out, I have read Russian newspapers and kept in touch with some of the child care staff and parents I met while I was in Moscow. In December of 1993 I telephoned center directors with questions about changes in their centers since 1991. This chapter briefly describes what I have learned. A few general words about the national scene are followed by some information specific to the centers I visited.

In December of 1991 I spoke briefly to Dr. Nikita Schklovsky, of the Ministry of Health, during one of his visits to the United States. Exaggerating to make his point, he predicted that in a few years child care for children under the age of 6 would be no more in Russia. "We can't afford it," he said. In fact, many child care centers across the nation have indeed closed their doors. There are no longer any *yasli* to speak of; center-based infant care is no longer available. Former *yasli* have either been converted to *yasli-sady*, providing care for children aged 1 1/2 to 6 years, or they have closed entirely. As costs have risen and funding from public sources and sponsoring organizations has not kept pace, many centers that once served preschoolers aged 3 to 6 have also closed. Those that remain have drastically raised the fees parents must pay. Frequently I read stories in the Russian press about the hardships these closings and fee raises impose on parents ("Detsad," 1993; "Detstvo," 1991; "Men'she," 1992). New private centers accommodate some of the children who would have attended the closed centers, but there are too few of them, and often their fees are too expensive for the average family ("Detsad," 1993).

Child care staff have suffered in other ways too. Inflation-corrected wages are now even lower than they were two years ago, and upbringers earn less than half the average Russian wage (Shapiro, 1993). To compound the insult, as more lucrative careers have opened up in the commercial realm, the prestige of low-paying employment, including that in the child care field, has fallen (Akimova, 1993).

It should come as no surprise that the quality of care offered in some centers has also been negatively affected. The family-oriented newspaper *Sem'ia* has carried pleas from child care center directors for donations of toys from the public (e.g., "Pomozhem!" 1992). This newspaper has also reported on centers that have reduced the number of health checks for child care center staff from four times to once annually ("Niania," 1993), have reduced the amount of food served at mealtimes (only the first *or* the second course is served for lunch), and/or have begun requiring children to bring their own bedding, toys, and even dishes ("Golod," 1991). Some centers now charge parents extra for lessons in music and physical education ("Samoe dorogoe," 1993). As a money-making venture, other centers offer, for a supplementary fee, lessons in foreign languages (English is a favorite). One mother told me that, in her opinion, these supplementary lessons are of low quality; I wonder also about the feelings of children whose parents cannot afford the additional fee.

Positive things are happening also. The picture is not entirely grim. Already in 1991, I read and heard about experimental preschool programs designed to foster inquisitiveness, independent problem-solving ability, and creativity in children (e.g., Nikitina, 1990). A curriculum called *Raduga* (Rainbow) was gaining popularity. This program encourages upbringers to integrate the five lesson areas and to incorporate opportunities for music, creativity, and problem solving into all aspects of the daily routine (see, for example, Tzarkova & Serbina, 1993). The atmosphere is to be warm, and both children and adults are to have opportunities to make choices and initiate activities. Interest in such programs is high, and staff now have the freedom to try them.

What about the centers I visited? Were there any changes since I had observed? "Nothing is different. It is all the same," was two directors' first response to my question. After some probing, I found out that some important changes had, in fact, occurred, but what had stayed the same was also significant. First, all of the metro-sponsored centers have survived the nation's recent economic storms, and they are still funded by the (renamed) Department of Transportation Networks. The two *yasli* have been converted to *yasli-sady* accommodating children from 1 1/2 to 5 years of age. Group sizes and ratios of adults to children are exactly as before. Staff members still receive the perks described in Chapter 3. The system of inspections from external agencies has not changed. "A lot has happened in our *country*," one director told me, "but in our center everything, everything is the same."

"How is the food?" I asked, remembering that this was a source of concern when I was there last. "Good. Maybe even better than when you were here because the city of Moscow gives us a food subsidy," was the unexpected answer. Since one of the perks awarded for working for the metro-system-sponsored child care centers is free meals while on the job, the improved quality of food must have special meaning for staff.

Directors did mention that parents' fees have increased a great deal but noted that their centers are nevertheless filled to capacity. One director explained that maternity leave subsidies are too low to allow most mothers to stay home with young children, so demand for center care is high. An unfortunate sign of the times is that many parents are picking children up very late, after 6:30. "Is it because they know their children will be fed dinner if they stay late?" I asked. The answers suggested that dinner might have something to do with it; the main reason though was that parents were exhausted and used the time between work and picking up their children to rest and/or do necessary shopping.

In some centers important changes are occurring in curriculum. First, upbringers may now decide on lesson plans themselves. No one tells them exactly what to do and how to do it. Curriculum specialists, one director told me, are now regarded as helpers; their role is no longer that of the feared inspector. Even more importantly, some directors are excited about the new curricula (Raduga was specifically mentioned) that encourage creativity and independent problem solving in children. There are many new manuals out with ideas for upbringers who wish to foster these qualities in children. One director explained that, whereas before upbringers showed children exactly what to do and showed them models that they were to copy, now they give children only the outline of a problem or project and ask them to figure out their own solutions themselves. As readers of Chapters 8 and 9 of this book will surely appreciate, this new approach to lessons represents a radical change for many upbringers (and children as well) and must be difficult to implement.

Probing for more information, I asked if the daily routine had changed in the centers. The answer to this question was more interesting than I would have predicted. As it turns out, in 1992 many of the centers decided to do away with lessons altogether. Thinking them too adult-directed and too divorced from the rest of the day, directors and upbringers decided instead to incorporate the five areas that had been the focus of lessons into indoor and outdoor free play times. (As I listened, I couldn't help but think of the radical experiments of the 1920s, when traditional educational practices were thrown out in favor of Western-style "free upbringing" philosophies. See Chapter 2.)

Within months, however, the staff became disenchanted with the loose schedule. They felt that children were not learning all that they should and that their intellectual levels and physical fitness had declined. In 1993, at a national conference of curriculum specialists working for centers associated with railroads (the Moscow metro-sponsored centers are part of this system), it was decided to reinstitute the daily routine as it was before (and as it is described in this book in Chapter 6). The directors I spoke to were pleased at this reversal. "After all, our pedagogues of the past understood many things well. We shouldn't throw out everything," said one.

Another change has been in playroom arrangement. Recall that at the time of my visit, shelves and other equipment and toys were placed around the perimeter of playrooms, leaving a large open space in the center. At least one director has now used various room dividers (chairs, shelves, tables) to create "zones" in the playrooms in her center. Each zone is akin to what American teachers know as an "interest area." The director who spoke to me about this indicated that the zones seem to help children feel more secure and calm; children decide which zone they wish to play in and then are not distracted by the goings-on of children in the other zones in the room. "There is less squabbling among children. Also they do less running in the playroom now. They don't need to run indoors; they have plenty of time outside to run."

Outside, the play yard is still divided so that groups do not mix. One director happily told me that she had been able to purchase new bushes and fir trees and was using them as dividers to better separate the different groups' play areas.

This led me to questions about goals for children. The answers were similar to those I had heard two years before: the foremost goal of child care is still the development of kindness and the ability to have positive relationships with others. At least one director felt successful in this regard. "The children are wonderful. They get along with each other better than ever. They are not jealous and they don't bicker the way the adults do. Adult relationships are so difficult now; people are on edge and not as considerate of each other as before. But these problems don't seem to affect the children. It is a joy to watch them. Even when their parents pick them up late, they are happy and play together well," she said. I was interested to hear this, particularly in light of a letter I received a year ago from the director of another center telling me that children seemed sadder, more worried, than before. The first director seemed to attribute the well-being of the children in her center to the new style of lessons and to the introduction of zones in the playrooms.

Regarding child-rearing goals, I was also told that there is more emphasis now on intellectual development, particularly on the development of logic. New children's books that teach concepts in geography, biology, ecology, and art are being used. One director has made it a priority to acquire folk art, so that children can be exposed to the history of their culture. She told me that these items are now more available and cheaper than they used to be. Parents are chipping in to help purchase them. Again, the same director who thought children's social skills were better than ever also thought they were coming to her center intellectually very well prepared. "It is not unusual to have 3-year-olds who read," she said. When I expressed amazement, she remarked that maybe it has something to do with the kind of parents who send their children to her center.

Another change is the observance of Christian holidays. Centers are now closed for Christmas as well as for New Years Day, and both are celebrated with special children's performances. One director is especially looking forward to Shrovetide in February. As she has for the past two years, in 1994 she will hire a horse and buggy to give the children rides. Afterward they will sip hot tea outdoors while singing and listening to music.

One last change has to do with performance evaluations of upbringers. Recall, from Chapter 3, that in 1991 upbringers were preparing for a new system dividing them into "categories." Salaries were to be commensurate with the rankings they earned. This system has been put into effect and is, in itself, a major change from pre-*perestroika* days.

What did the directors want for the future? Interest in innovative programming fostering creativity and independent problem solving seems to be high; directors are learning about curricula that support these goals and deciding which ones they would like to adopt for their centers.

In another vein, one director told me that she had visited a private child care center that enrolls 6- and 7-year-olds and provides them with first- and second-grade schooling. This kind of programming is attractive for parents because all-day care is included and because there is a widespread perception that public schools are overcrowded and developmentally inappropriate for young children. This director would like to include first- and second-grade curricula in her center also, if only she could find the money. She would also like to hire a psychologist and a physical education specialist for her center but currently lacks sufficient funding. So far her appeals to the Department of Transportation Networks have been unsuccessful. (Another director has approached the problem differently; when she wanted to offer English lessons, she simply asked parents to pay extra if they wanted their children to participate.)

All in all, my telephone conversations left me with a better feeling than I had gained from press reports. Much of that, of course, has to do with the special nature of the centers I visited. The reader will recall from upbringers' and directors' comments quoted throughout this book, and especially in Chapters 4 and 14, that most of the them were decidedly interested in "democratizing" their programs. For them, there is excitement in present opportunities.

The one sobering note came when I called a child care center and was told that the director would be out of town for a month. When I tried to engage the person who had answered the telephone in conversation, she politely asked me to call back when the director returned. "Could you just tell me if your center now enrolls preschool-aged children as well as toddlers?" I persisted. (This center had been a *yasli* before.) "Please, you will have to ask the director," was the reply. Hanging up, I felt reminded of the fear of authority (and foreigners) instilled by decades of Soviet rule. It has not disappeared.

Indeed, child care professionals in Russia face many challenges as well as many opportunities. In the years to come it will be fascinating to continue to follow their paths.

References

Akimova, L. (1993, November 22-28). Sel'skaia uchitel'nitsa [Rural teacher]. *Sem'ia*, No. 47, pp. 4-5.

Alekseeva, A. S., Druzhinina, L. V., & Ladodo, K. S. (1990). *Organizatsiia Pitaniia Detei v Doshkol'nyh Uchrezhdeniiah* [Organization of Children's Nutrition in Preschool Facilities]. Moscow: Prosveshchenie.

Amid economic chaos, health of Russia's people deteriorates. (1992, August 23), *St. Louis Post-Dispatch*, p. 7B.

Andreeva, V. N., & Khukhlaeva, D. V. (1986). Fizicheskoe vospitanie [Physical upbringing]. In L. V. Russkova (Ed.), *Metodicheskie Rekomendatsii k "Programme Vospitaniia i Obucheniia v Detskom Sadu"* (pp. 116-153). Moscow: Prosveshchenie.

Avdeeva, K. (1992, May 18-24). Nadoelo byt' rabyniami! [Tired of being slaves!]. *Sem'ia*, No. 20, p. 6.

Baumrind, D. (1967). Child care practices anteceding three patterns of preschool behavior. *Genetic Psychology Monographs, 75*, 43-88.

Bereday, G. Z. F., Brickman, W. W., & Read, G. H. (1960). *The Changing Soviet School*. Cambridge, MS: Riverside Press.

Black, R. (1992, November). The 10 best daycare centers in America. *Child*, pp. 154-161.

Bogina, T. L., & Terekhova, N. T. (1987). *Rezhim Dnia v Detskom Sadu* [The Daily Routine in the Preschool]. Moscow: Prosveshchenie.

Boguslavskaia, Z. M., & Smirnova, E. O. (1991). *Razvivaiushchie Igry dlia Detei Mladshego Doshkol'novo Vozrasta* [Developmental

Games for Children of Early Preschool Age]. Moscow: Prosveshchenie.

Bondarenko, A. K., & Voronova, V. Y. (1986). Igra [Play]. In L. V. Russkova (Ed.), *Metodicheskie Rekomendatsii k "Programme Vospitania i Obychenie v Detskom Sadu"* (pp. 53-81). Moscow: Prosveshchenie.

Bredekamp, S. (1987). *Developmentally Appropriate Practice in Early Childhood Programs Serving Children from Birth through Age 8.* Washington, D.C.: NAEYC.

Brickman, W. (1972). Chronological outline of Soviet education. *School and Society, 100,* pp. 253-259.

Brittain, W. L. (1979). *Creativity, Art, and Young Children.* New York: Macmillan.

Bronfenbrenner, U. (1970a). Reaction to social pressure from adults versus peers among Soviet day school and boarding school pupils in the perspective of an American sample. *Journal of Personality and Social Psychology, 15,* 179-189.

Bronfenbrenner, U. (1970b). *Two Worlds of Childhood: U.S. and U.S.S.R.* New York: Russell Sage Foundation.

Butsinskaia, P. P., Vasiukova, V. I., & Leskova, G. P. (1990). *Obshcherazvivaiiushchie Uprazhneniia v Detskom Sadu* [Exercises for Overall Development in the Preschool]. Moscow: Prosveshchenie.

Chybarov, L. (1966). Organizatsia collectiva [Organization of the collective]. In L. Chybarov (Ed.), *Shtobi Ros Chelovek* (p. 24). Moscow: Molodaia Gvardia.

Danilova, V. V., & Piskareva, N. A. (1986). Razvitie elementarnykh matematicheskikh predstavlenii. [The development of elementary mathematical concepts]. In L. V. Russkova (Ed.), *Metodicheskie Rekomendatsii k "Programme Vospitania i Obychenie v Detskom Sadu"* (pp. 256-291). Moscow: Prosveshchenie.

Detsad zakryt: Vse ushli na zarabotki [The preschool is closed: Everyone left to make money]. (1993, August 9-15), *Sem'ia,* No. 32, p. 3.

Detstvo—s molotka [Childhood—with a hammer]. (1991, November 18-24), *Sem'ia,* No. 47, p. 2.

Dinkmeyer, D., McKay, G., & Dinkmeyer, D. (1990). *Systematic Training for Effective Teaching.* Circle Pines, MN: American Guidance Service.

Dlia vas—on edinstvennyi [For you—he's the only one]. (1993, November 15-21), *Sem'ia,* No. 46, p. 8.

Doronova, T. N., & Yakobson, S. G. (1992). *Obychenie Detei 2-4 Let Ricovaniiu, Lepke, Applikatsii v Igre* [Teaching 2- To 4-year-old Children Drawing, Sculpture, and Applique within Play]. Moscow: Prosveshchenie.

Dunn, P. P. (1974). "That enemy is the baby": Childhood in Imperial Russia. In L. deMause (Ed.), *The History of Childhood* (pp. 383-405). New York: Psychohistory Press.

Edwards, L. C., & Nabors, M. L. (1993). The creative arts process: What it is and what it is not. *Young Children, 48*, 77-81.

Engels, F. *The Origin of the Family, Private Property and the State.* New York: International Publishers, 1967. (Original work published in 1884.)

Gartrell, D. (1987). Punishment or guidance. *Young Children, 42*, 55-61.

Gerbova, V. V., Zimonina, V. N., & Pushnina, L. I. (1986). Oznakomlenie s okruzhaiushchim. Razvitie rechi. Oznakomlenie s proizvedeniami khudozhestvennoi literatury [Becoming familiar with the environment. Language development. Becoming familiar with fiction]. In L. V. Russkova (Ed.), *Metodicheskie Rekomendatsii k "Programme Vospitania i Obychenie v Detskom Sadu"* (pp. 153-256). Moscow: Prosveshchenie.

Golod v detskom sadu [Famine in the preschool]. (1991, May 13-19]. *Sem'ia*, No. 20, p. 2.

Gosstandart preduprezhdaet: Eda opasna dlia vashego zdorov'ia [The Office of Government Standards warns: Food is dangerous for your health]. (1993, July 12-18). *Sem'ia*, p. 3.

Gray, F. (1989). *Soviet Women: Walking the Tightrope.* New York: Doubleday.

Grebennikov, I. V., & Kovin'ko, L. V. (1990). *Semeinoe Vospitanie: Kratkii Slovar'* [Family Upbringing: A Short Dictionary]. Moscow: Politizdat.

Gribovskaia, A. A., Doronova, T. N., Khalezova, N. B., Chernik, T. V. (1986). Izobrazitel'naia deiatel'nost' [Representational activity]. In L. V. Russkova (Ed.), *Metodicheskie rekomendatsii k "Programme vospitaniia i obucheniia v detskom sadu"* (pp. 153-256). Moscow: Prosveshchenie.

Gribovskaia, A. A., Grigor'eva, I. P., Chernik, T. V., & Gerbova, V. V. (1986). Samostoiatel'naia khudozhestvennaia deiatel'nost' [Independent artistic activity]. In L. V. Russkova (Ed.), *Metodicheskie rekomendatsii k "Programme vospitaniia i obucheniia v detskom sadu"* (pp. 387-396). Moscow: Prosveshchenie.

Grigor'eva, I. P. (1986a). Muzykal'noe vospitanie [Musical up-bringing]. In L. V. Russkova (Ed.), *Metodicheskie rekomendatsii k "Programme vospitaniia i obucheniia v detskom sadu"* (pp. 366-383). Moscow: Prosveshchenie.

Grigor'eva, I. P. (1986b). Prazdniki i razvlechenia [Holidays and entertainment]. In L. V. Russkova (Ed.), *Metodicheskie rekomendatsii k "Programme vospitaniia i obucheniia v detskom sadu"* (pp. 383-386). Moscow: Prosveshchenie.

Hansson, C., & Liden, K. (1993). *Moscow Women*. New York: Pantheon.

Hildebrand, V. (1986). *Introduction to Early Childhood Education* (4th ed.). New York: Macmillan.

Hoffman, M. L. (1975). Moral internalization, parental power, and the nature of parent-child interaction. *Developmental Psychology, 11,* 228-239.

Hogan, E., Ispa, J. M., & Thornburg, K. R. (1992). Mother-provider interaction and the provider-child relationship in family child care homes. *Early Child Development and Care, 77,* 57-65.

Hohmann, M., Banet, B., Weikart, D. P. (1979). *Young Children in Action: A Manual for Preschool Educators*. Ypsilanti, MI: The High/Scope Press.

Hollingshead, A. (1975). *Four-factor Index of Social Status*. New Haven, CT: Yale University, Department of Sociology.

Ispa, J. M. (1977). The reactions of Soviet nursery day care and boarding care children to a strange situation. *Developmental Psychology, 13,* 421-422.

Ispa, J. M. (1988). Soviet immigrant mothers' perceptions regarding the first childbearing year: The 1950s and the 1970s. *Slavic Review, 47,* 291-306.

Ispa, J. M. (in press). Child-rearing ideas and feelings of Russian and American mothers and early childhood teachers: Some comparisons. *Advances in Early Education and Day Care*.

Jacoby, S. (December 4, 1973). Reforming Soviet education. *SR/World*, pp. 50-55.

Johnson, W. (1950). *Russia's Educational Heritage* (pp. 146-152). Pittsburgh, PA: Carnegie Press.

Komarova, T. (1990). Vospitatel' detskogo sada . . . kakim on dolzhen byt'? [The preschool teacher . . . what should he be like?] *Doshkol'noe Vospitanie, 3,* 5-7, 103.

Kononova, I. M. (1989). *Seminarskie i Prakticheskie Zaniatiia po Doshkol'noi Pedagogike* [Seminar And Practical Lessons In Preschool Education]. Moscow: Prosveshchenie.

Kontos, S., Raikes, H., & Woods, A. (1983). Early childhood staff attitudes toward their parent clientele. *Child Care Quarterly, 12,* 45-58.

About the Author

JEAN ISPA is Associate Professor of Human Development and Family Studies at the University of Missouri-Columbia. She has written *Exploring Careers in Child Care Services* (1984) now in its third edition.

ISBN 0-89789-390-5